The Beautiful Bride

...appraising contemporary church practice

Muyiwa Oguntoyinbo

The Beautiful Bride

Copyright: ©2010 Muyiwa Oguntoyinbo

Website: www.muyiwaoguntoyinbo.com
Email: contact@muyiwaoguntoyinbo.com
Blog: www.muyiwaoguntoyinbo.com/tbbBlog

ISBN: 978-0-9564927-1-5

Cover/Book design by: *Lacepoint Designs*

Published by:
Lacepoint Publishing
Website: www.lacapoint.ie
Email: services@lacepoint.ie
Telephone: +353 1 442 9971

All Scripture, unless otherwise stated, are taken from the New King James Version of the Bible. Copyright 1979, 1980, 1982, 1990, Thomas Nelson Inc.

All rights reserved under international Copyright law. This Book is a seed into the Kingdom of God. Hence contents may be reproduced in whole or in part in any form for non profit use, without the written consent of the Author, as long as the Author is credited and such actions are guarded by integrity and honour.

Printed in the Republic of Ireland.

CONTENTS

Foreword · · · · · 5
Acknowledgement · · · · · 9
Introduction · · · · · 11

CHAPTER ONE: · · · · · 13
The Ancient Path

CHAPTER TWO: · · · · · 49
Church and Money

CHAPTER THREE: · · · · · 73
What is wrong with Clergy?

CHAPTER FOUR: · · · · · 103
Monuments or Church?

CHAPTER FIVE: · · · · · 123
The Bride and Groom

CHAPTER SIX: · · · · · 149
To whom shall we go?

Foreword

And I say also unto thee, That thou art Peter, and upon this rock I will build my church; and the gates of hell shall not prevail against it. (Matt. 16: 18)

Notice that the above passage guarantees the church's victory over Satan and his kingdom but not that we would not suffer bruises. Our "good success" in any endeavor comes by a strict adherence to the word of God (Jos. 1:8). The gospel of Christ — or the word of God is God's power to salvation in anything, anywhere.

In terms of victory, the church is vibrant and taking territories; there is no better time to live as a Christian than now. The knowledge of the word of God in the church have increased, available facilities for the work of God is staggering; we are blessed with powerful men and well-endowed women. When it also comes to bruises, we have not a few. There is no time in history when the church is more frivolous, more worldly, more corky and self-conceited than now. We have success and victories but with character problems.

Moreover, who we are is by far more important than what we can ever achieve; this is because Ps 116:15 says that God has given the earth to mankind; He has also decided to reveal Himself through His people on earth. He is also a principled personality that honors His word. Therefore, when we fail His word, we send wrong signals to unbelievers about Him.

The church therefore needs a rapid and constant diagnostic appraisal of itself to correct and reposition itself in line with the word of God. In doing that we must not lose sight of the grounds taken and success achieved lest we become discouraged, but we must also not indulge ourselves or be self-conceited.

However, analysis of our problems is tougher than you think; in fact, each time you focus the camera on the problems the lens cracks! And it is for two major reasons. Firstly, success is a two-edged sword that confirms both truth and errors. I have heard so-called mega Pastors say boldly that one shouldn't listen to someone that is not doing better. A Pastor and Televangelist once said that his critics only want to "minimize him in order to level up". Once they succeed, they also stop learning.

Secondly, many of our strengths double as our weaknesses. Take the issue of prosperity for example, God surely wants us to live well and enjoy plenty; however even Israel was warned not to forget God in prosperity which of course they failed to do. There is also a thin line separating prosperity from greediness. What is your take on a man of God that owns twenty luxury cars and lives in opulence but has no charity programme to bless the poor even in his local church? Or those that equate material acquisition to levels of faith?

Well, to balance this some had also gone off balance attacking prosperity in its entirety and in fact, in many cases advocating for poverty. Prosperity then is a strong point of the Church; a poor church covered with sores like Lazarus and begging bread cannot reflect God's glory, cannot fulfill the great commission and will not portray God as a responsible father. Sadly, prosperity is also our weak point; an obese church cannot run the race, a gluttonous church cannot fast and pray, a materialistic church builds empires on earth, is arrogant and self-seeking.

This is the murky water Muyiwa Oguntoyinbo has dabbled into in this work and I salute his courage. He has written this timely book from the standpoint of a passenger and scholar; even though he was an assistant Pastor for some years. I am not surprised if you disagree with observations and postulations in this book; it is the terrain. But be sure to side with the truth and disagree in good conscience. Truth has a million lives and will always resurrect; your conscience may be "seared with hot iron" but it is God's witness and secret police that has a role to play in the coming judgment (Rom.2: 14-16). Therefore, as each of our problems comes under focus, if you elect to crack the lens kindly make sure not to crack your conscience as well; doing so is tantamount to holding the truth in unrighteousness (Rom. 1: 18). Of course, the lens may waste away but truth and conscience shall be there hereafter; to confront you or stand with you. Your position and attitude today is the decider.

Recommending this book to every Christian, I want to leave you with a Hebrew proverb, "Truth is heavy; only a few carry it".

Rev. Emmanuel Baba-Lola

Dublin, June 2010.

From the Author's desk

A mere 'acknowledgement' on this page does not seem adequate for the God of all ages, whose I am. He deserves glory, honour and praise, as the One to whom I owe grace and inspiration for writing.

I am privileged to be married to Adetoro Oguntoyinbo, my treasured friend and the most supportive person I know on earth. Thanks for taking time to pray along with me and for being a true friend. Your objective feedback on this piece has been of tremendous benefit.

Special thanks to my friend and sister, Kemi Owolabi for a thorough walk-through of the manuscript. Your words of encouragement through the lifespan of the project are invaluable. You are a rare gem!

I am also extremely grateful to wonderful friends – Daniel Egurube, Chidinma Odibeli and Ibiene Oguntoyinbo for reviewing the manuscript. Thanks for your great assistance in correcting my grammar. This work wouldn't have been complete without your inputs and I am confident that the Lord will reward you.

It is imperative that I salute my mentor, Rev Emmanuel Baba-Lola for his advice and detailed review of this book. I strongly agree with Paul, the Apostle that though we have many instructors in the Lord, there are not many fathers. The largeness of your heart, your deep spiritual insights and sound coaching abilities distinguish you as a servant-leader in this generation.

Again, I am conscious to return all glory to God. He is the Kingdom Project Manager and Custodian of wisdom, and I am only a resource in His Hands.

Introduction

I recently had discussions with a friend who is a pastor of a fairly new church in London and he explained God's plan to me with words that linger in my memory as I write this book. His words were "......*a silent revolution has started....*" Those words encapsulate the thoughts I had nursed in my heart many months before our discussion.

This book is a compilation of various observations about Christ's church and how present day practices tally with scriptural antecedents. Jesus established the church to occupy spiritual and terrestrial territories, dismantle evil devices, pronounce Christ's Lordship and earnestly prepare for the Lord's return.

This book will challenge you to take your God-given right in Christ. It will open up age-long truth in new dimensions and steer our hearts in the direction of God's plan for His church. If you have questioned the status quo for a very long time, then this book was written with you in mind. If you have become weary from religion and yearn for a deeper understanding of God's ways, this book was written to shine God's light onto your path. There is a lot more to the Christian experience than what the gigantic monument called church currently offers. There is liberty in God, and He expects us to walk in that liberty.

I submit this piece to the scrutiny of every child of God who is hungry for the truth. I do not lay claim to perfection or monopoly of God's mind. Instead, I am subject to my brethren and request that you study the material in your hands under the guidance of God's Spirit. I have deliberately left out names in this book but if any of the persons referred to are identifiable, please note that the purpose is not to cast aspersions on any one.

I invite you to travel along with me as we unmask satan's wicked plots in keeping the church weak. Please read this book with an open mind. You may consider holding a bible close by to cross check the points raised therein. Jesus loves his beautiful bride deeply. He will no doubt lead us back to the foot of the cross, and restore the glory of His resurrection.......if only we are willing and desperate for His fullness.

Muyiwa Oguntoyinbo

The Ancient Path

Lord, we confess that we have wandered
Far from your purpose and plan
And willingly walked in the wrong direction
We've disobeyed Your commands
Father forgive us, Spirit come lead us
Back to the way, back to the truth
Back to the foot of the cross

Show us the ancient paths
Lead us along eternal highways
We want to walk in the ways of Jesus
We want to enter Your rest
Show us the ancient paths
Lead us along eternal highways
We want to follow the footsteps of Jesus
We want to enter your rest
(Song written by Tom Inglis)

That morning, He looked at the crowd and announced His departure in a most reassuring way. Some had previously expressed concerns about his planned separation from them but on this particular day, His words reverberated with so much love and drove home a compelling message. *"For Lo, I am with you till the end of the age"*. Those words are as important today as they were when spoken over two thousand years ago. The Man at the centre stage, Jesus

Christ departed leaving behind The Church – the ecclesia: a people that belong to Him, a different kind of people, a people that represent Him and reflect His presence. Such a huge responsibility! Little wonder then that Jesus asked the church to wait for the Holy Spirit's infilling before stepping into ministry. May we find fulfilment at being satisfied as His vessels who express His image on earth. No better time than now.

> *The journey of the church began by the infilling of the Holy Spirit. A special people then began to multiply on the earth at an alarming rate.*

What an irony. A Man gives a farewell message and yet promises to stay back. What was Jesus really saying? Why would He depart and yet say *"I am with you"*? Did He mean what He said? No doubt, He did. Upon Jesus' separation from the people, the church was spurned out. A journey began. A trail was blazed in the Acts 2 infilling experience and today, the church is still on that long journey. The mind of Christ when He promised His presence is that the church would have all of Him and be His manifestation on the earth. In a functional body, the head and the body are fitly joined. The head sends signals to the body and the body responds without debate. They are one! They are always in agreement. So, the real message Jesus conveyed in that farewell speech was this: "Take all of Me and be Me on the earth, and continue like that always until I return for you".

As already mentioned and as is widely known, the journey of the church began by the infilling of the Holy Spirit. A special people then began to multiply on the earth at an alarming rate. These were a people that did not deliberately draw attention to themselves yet they could not be ignored by society, religious leaders or the government. They operated at such an unstoppable force and stayed bound together in love. Success and failure were communal as the believing community shared the Master's Life. The church, though at its infancy began to take shape quickly and we learnt important lessons about the mind of Christ, and about His body, from the nature of the church soon after the Lord's physical departure from the earth.

The 1st century church was a landmark phenomenon. That church is still an example simply because the church personified Jesus through her daily operations. Church was family indeed and relationships were not superficial. Through thick and thin, this new family found commonality - their relationship with Jesus Christ. Thus, they expressed His love to one another. Fellowship was true to the word. There is something peculiar about the first century church. There were Elders, Apostolic workers and Deacons but there were no "super-stars". The Lord expressed Himself through everyone that was available to Him. The church was on a mission and was passionate about assignment.

All of church expressed the nature of Christ and this was inclusive of the entire believing community. The church expressed power, not a few "stars". The church was prominent, not a special class in church. These attributes of the first century church are significant.

A lot has changed since this ancient path was charted in the first century. Most of what we call church today is departure from the apostolic order, passed down from first century church. What has gone wrong? Will the church ever return to the ancient path?

In this chapter, we shall examine the basic departure from 1st century church practice. The aim is to ensure we collectively find our way back to the Master's plan of being His able representatives on the earth. But first, let's start with the excellent things the church has accomplished.

THE BEAUTY OF CHURCH

As already established, the church launched out in the power of the Holy Spirit with 120 people. That figure later became 3,120 in one day and the growth has been astronomical since then. The beautiful bride of the Lord began to take bold steps towards establishing the nature and character of the Master Jesus on earth. The church took huge strides in destiny. She leaped walls of opposition erected by the Jewish religious order and the fierce Roman government. Twenty centuries later, the church continues to flourish despite the countless persecutions she encountered in this long journey. The following points highlight some of the achievements of the church through the ages, albeit this list is by no means exhaustive:

- <u>Persecution</u>: From inception, the church was greeted with hostility. In Jerusalem, so great was the persecution that Christians had to travel to distant regions or be killed. But that is not all with persecution. Today, the church continues to suffer persecution in many Nations of the earth. Believers are not always liked for saying the truth yet the church continues to boldly declare allegiance to the Name of the Lord, Jesus. Many have died in prisons and many still secretly hold church meetings in certain countries where the gospel is banned, yet the church continues to thrive. In the truest sense of the word, the beautiful bride of Jesus has endured untold hardship. The church has gracefully embraced persecution as a catalyst for spiritual and numerical growth.
- <u>Charity</u>: The church has made notable contributions to society as we know it today. In many countries of the world and until recently, churches assumed the responsibility of building schools for free education. Churches established hospitals and other social amenities, and provided most of these services at no cost to the beneficiaries. This is simply noble and laudable!
- <u>Global Evangelism</u>: Today, many nations of the earth have heard the salvation message of Jesus Christ because Christian missionaries were faithful to the great commission, right in the face of adversity. Many submitted their rights to live comfortable lives and chose to rather suffer in remote under-developed villages, just to fulfil the Lord's call upon their lives and spread His love to humanity. I have read touching

stories of missionaries who lost so much to ensure the message of the cross reaches the ends of the earth. Many lost their lives in the process.

- <u>Social Reformation</u>: In many instances, church hasn't been docile in political matters of the world. The church has over time realised her responsibilities over the earth thus many Christian leaders have spoken out publicly against social injustice. At this juncture, I pay tribute to late Rev Martin Luther king (Jnr) for his resolute fight against injustice in America. Many other Christians have fulfilled the Masters' heartbeat about bearing each others' burden and speaking for the downtrodden. Some others have enforced righteous governance by preaching to kings and presidents, and in some cases mentoring them. The church has set high moral standards and she checks the conscience of society by being fearlessly outspoken.

On all of these remarkable achievements, I salute the church and her leadership. Surely, heaven has these and many other secret good works on record, and commensurate reward for all those who sacrificed to attain these heights will be revealed in eternity.

However, we still have a lot to attain in God's eternal purpose and we shall be examining many areas of improvements in this book.

THE FUNDAMENTAL TRUTH!

1 Pet 2: 9-10
But you are a chosen generation, a royal priesthood, a holy nation, His own special people, that you may proclaim the praises of Him who called you out of darkness into His marvellous light; who once were not a people but are now the people of God, who had not obtained mercy but now have obtained mercy.

Clearly, the church is made of kings and priests. Royalty flows in our blood streams and by genetic make-up, all true believers are joint heirs with Christ. This ageless truth is constant from generation to generation. Christ's church is not made of different categories of believers. In Romans 8:17, Paul described Jesus as the first born among many brethren, thus all believers are on the same plane. Only Jesus occupies the unique position of First Born, Husband, Lord, King to the church. For emphasis, that needs repetition. All believers, regardless of spiritual experiences, doctrinal beliefs, gifts and spiritual depths, are equal! A pastor, an elder, a bishop and a new believer share the same position in Christ. They are brethren! This goes against the notion permeating the 21st Century church, where adulation and inordinate accordance are heaped on ministers and servants of God. There is no super human, just as there is no super star in God's royal family. All sinned, and all require repentance for acceptance into God's family. No man therefore owns an exclusive right to God, neither is any man superior to another man. This is foundational truth and is not often taught in church today. Some "men of God" would rather have people believe they are some sort of intermediaries to God. Nothing can be farther from the truth. There is one God, and one Mediator between

God and man, the Man Christ Jesus (1 Tim 2:5). That a man can express spiritual gifts doesn't make him superior. He is still a frail man and as James, the Apostle likes to call such heroes of faith – a man of like passion. Such man, through his hunger for righteousness and unusual love for God, may experience God at a deeper level than other believers yet that does not place him as a superior being from God's perspective.

Examination of the New Testament church practice shows that no special class within the body ever existed until sometime around the 2nd century. According to Frank Viola's and George Barna's *Pagan Christianity*, the church took example from its surrounding environment – the world:

Church leadership began to formalise at about the time of the death of the itinerant apostolic workers (church planters). In the late first and early second centuries, local presbyters began to emerge as the resident "successors" to the unique leadership role played by the apostolic workers. This gave rise to a single leading figure in early church. Without the influence of the extra-local workers who had been mentored by the New Testament apostles, the church began to drift towards the organisational patterns of her surrounding culture.

The class system within the body is destructive and is not a reflection of God's plan for His church. Read Titus 2:14

....who gave Himself for us, that He might redeem us from every lawless deed and purify for Himself His own special people zealous for good works.

God's desire has always been to have a peculiar or special people He can call His own on the earth. It is for this reason He originally desired the Nation of Israel to be that special people – a nation of priests.

Ex 19: 5-6
Now therefore, if you will indeed obey My voice and keep My covenant, then you shall be a treasure to Me above all people; for all the earth is Mine. <u>And you shall be to Me a kingdom of priests and a holy nation</u>. These are the words which you shall speak to the children of Israel.

God's ultimate goal is clear in this scripture – Israel was to be special, a people that had direct access to Him as priests. When Israel failed to meet that expectation by keeping the condition in verse 5, God then chose the tribe of Levi as His special tribe of priests, a shadow of the superior priesthood to come when Christ is revealed. Levitical priesthood was a temporary measure and not God's ultimate solution in meeting His desire for a nation that would be directly accountable to Him. It is therefore not a surprise that He greatly frowned at Israel's rejection of His direct rule during the days of Samuel. Today, God desires a nation that will express the nature of His Son on the earth today. Salvation is not the ultimate goal in divine agenda; it is instead the starting point. As Paul explains it, until we come to the full measure of the Person of Christ, the renewal work in man will continue.

> *Ministry is mutually inclusive and must be participatory in delivery.*

Based on this, wherever the 'five-fold' ministry is exalted above measure, something is wrong. Indeed, the Lord gave gifts to men to enable the entire body function as one whole piece but the gifts and assignments do not supersede the divine mandate that the kingdom structure should remain flat. That you are a pastor does not make you superior over a brother whose assignment in the Lord is somewhat invisible or at the background. The concept of five-fold ministry has over the years translated into a stronghold and an exclusive group in the body. In fact, some Christian groups have defined reward systems around the notion that a select group within the body will continue to "officiate" while others passively watch. This is faulty! It is abnormal and entirely foreign to first century church practice. Christian fellowship is all-inclusive, participative and organic in nature. Any alteration to that is a departure from the truth. Needless to say then, that any church exalting a special class of people above others in the church has departed from the truth. Ministry is mutually inclusive and must be participatory in delivery. For instance, brethren with teaching gifts should be allowed to express their gifts whether they are "ordained" into ministry or not. What obtains today is that a brother or sister with a teaching gift is not allowed to "share pulpit" with the sole pastor and in frustration "receives" a call to start another church. Saints, this breaks God's heart (especially because of the disaffection such separations lead to).

While still on the subject of equality between saints, it is imperative we address another problem prevalent in Christ's body today and which also flows from the warped mentality that a superior special class is acceptable to God. As a reader of this book, you may have heard that some "pastors" have special powers to curse their members. That is scripturally baseless and completely unfounded. Only Christ who paid the ultimate sacrifice for sin has the power to judge, approve or condemn. (In any event, a true child of God will not take pleasure in cursing). Read Romans 8: 33-34:

Who shall bring a charge against God's elect? It is God who justifies. Who is he who condemns? It is Christ who died, and furthermore is also risen, who is even at the right hand of God, who also makes intercession for us.

Notice Paul's link between condemnation and intercession. While Jesus holds the exclusive right to condemn, He does not exercise that right yet. Instead, He intercedes right there at the right hand of God. Christ's new law is that of true love and I dare say that anyone who curses at will does not know the heart of God. There are pastors who threaten to curse church members over unresolved differences. This absurdity has no place in Christ's church.

STARDOM

The issue of equality between saints leads me to another issue. This is the celebrity status pervading the class of people that the church has come to accept as special. They bear different types of titles, and some of these titles are self-acclaimed positions that have nothing to do with heaven's recognition. Is there anything wrong with being popular? Not at all! The problem starts when you crave to be popular and scheme your way to it. Come to think of it, Jesus wasn't popular. He was famous but his opinions were at odds with the religious order of His day and He was not an accepted man in society. What do we see today? Church leaders are now celebrities who are in popular demand to speak what the world wants to hear. They receive awards from governments and are considered as friends.

Another trend is that preachers and renowned "men of God" deliberately draw a lot of attention to themselves. Let us examine a scripture that counters this practice.

Matt 9: 30
And their eyes were opened. And Jesus sternly warned them, saying "see that no one knows it"

> *A true servant of the Lord must be prepared to be uncelebrated and ignored.*

Jesus was not an attention seeker. He had what the world needed and the world came looking for Him, but not once did He crave attention or popularity. The Jesus I know is one that would rather divert attention from Him to focus in prayer. He would rather do the miracles silently and not be noticed. Today, almost every pastor has a message that must be transmitted by mass media. Almost every preacher believes he/she has a "global platform". Almost every "man of God" has God's message for the entire globe and must be seen on TV. Surely, this is a case of misplaced priorities. If we are following Jesus, why would we draw attention to ourselves if Jesus didn't? An average pastor or reverend gentleman attends an event and expects that as part of normal protocol, he must be recognised or if possible made to speak. On the contrary, when Mary diverted attention to Jesus at a public function - the wedding of Cana, He frowned at it. It is not on record that Jesus ever demanded attention or public recognition. He inevitably got the attention because of His revolutionist stand but not because He schemed his way into popularity. A person who is offended that he is not accorded the recognition deserved at a public function does not know the Lord enough. If a pastor is offended that he was not greeted with respect, then it calls to question the spiritual maturity of such a person. Some even expect their Bibles to be collected from them as a mark of honour. While there is nothing specifically wrong with that except where it is demanded, if a pastor has no physical disability, then he should carry his bible himself! A true servant of the Lord must be prepared to be uncelebrated and ignored. He should receive ridicule as part of the package, bearing in mind that the real reward for service in the Lord's vineyard is what eternity will unveil.

I am aware modern day preachers admonish Christians to only visit places they are celebrated. What business then did Jesus have with Jerusalem, the city that initially welcomed him but turned around to mock, reject and crucify Him? While it is good to be celebrated, we mustn't become addicted to people's approval. If Jesus only yearned for celebration, would He have died the shameful death of the cross? The writer of Hebrews mentioned that He endured the cross and despised its shame. What message do we preach when we tell people that life is only about being celebrated and accepted? Certainly, that is not the message of the cross. Read the words of the Master: John 15: 19-20; *If you were of the world, the world would love its own. Yet because you are not of the world, but I chose you out of the world, therefore the world hates you. Remember the word that I said to you, 'A servant is not greater than his master'. If they persecuted Me, they will also persecute you. If they kept My word, they will keep yours also.*

SECRET WORK

A true child of God should be prepared to work in the background, unnoticed and unrecognised. In the real sense of faith, what eternity reveals is what truly matters to God. A man therefore should look towards eternity for rewards. No wonder then that Jesus reviled the Pharisees who engaged in public show of good works. Personally, I believe that we should only see a fraction of a Christian's good works on earth. A bulk of the good works you do as a Christian should be done in secret so that the good Lord will reward you openly. The best open reward is what eternity reveals because all mankind will see it together. There should be a surprise element to your life when we stand before God in judgement. That should be our goal as true believers. There is therefore no need to advertise our good works on radio, TV and colourful magazines. Our charitable deeds do not need to be known by men. Jesus frowned at that notion and He still does.

> *Let me indicate clearly that money is good and important. It is however only a means and not an end.*

This needs to be balanced appropriately:

Matthew 5:16
Let your light so shine before men, that they may see your good works and glorify your Father in heaven.

What was Jesus saying? In the preceding verse, He had announced to His hearers that they were the light of the world, and the salt of the earth. What does light do? It shines by nature. Jesus was saying, "be what you truly are and your works will announce whose child you are". This is the reason James, the Apostle described God as the "Father of lights".
So Jesus wasn't contradicting His warning to the Pharisees about secret good works. He was saying light needs no announcement by nature. According to John, light shines in darkness and darkness can't do anything contrary against it.

It then means Christians should shine in their daily interactions with the world. Shine in speech. Shine in kindness that is discharged through regular daily actions. Shining simply becomes a way of life and needs no separate announcement (unlike what the Pharisees were doing).

FINANCE

The subject of finance will be dealt with in greater measures in the next chapter. Money has been one of the most controversial issues church has been faced with, and that is no surprise. Money is a major force on the earth and has been for a long time. Jesus spoke a lot about money and at one point categorically warned that the god of money (mammon) was a direct rival of the Most High God (Matt 6:24)

Why is money a problem in church today? Was it an issue for the first century church? There are scriptural records that indicate so. Ananias and Saphirra were the first casualties of the spirit of greed, which functions through an attachment to mammon (Acts 5:1-11). This contest is rife in the 21st century but at greater intensity, and without doubt because there is more money today than the 1st century.

Let me indicate clearly that money is good and important. It is however only a means and not an end. While all churches would claim that money is not a motivating factor for establishment, it needs little exercise to prove that is incorrect. I am aware money causes rifts in churches. Some church splits are attempts to establish financial autonomy. If money was not central to the activities of such churches, why would it have such disastrous effects and break fellowships of believing saints? Money is crucial but it can play good or bad roles. It is good to remind ourselves that money can be a deadly tool in the hands of the enemy such that even Jesus was tempted with money (the third temptation about the glory of worldly kingdoms was money related. Matthew 4:8-9).

The main temptation with money is its intoxicating effect. Without restraint, money can dictate the pace of affairs in a community and thus assume the position of lord. A minister is under the influence of money when a bulk of his messages centres on money. Some ministers even claim that money is their "specialisation" in ministry. How appalling! Such people always cajole their members to give and expect to reap.

Over the years, I have observed preachers raise money in many interesting ways. Many of them share secrets of tried and tested methods and over time, the methods always seem to recur among different preachers. Some preachers tell their members to give a specific amount and link the amount to a numeric milestone, e.g. a specific year or a combination of month and year. Without mincing words, this is sentimentally motivated extortion.

The preachers that specialise on these methods of extortion apply sentiments and appeal to the emotions of gullible listeners. Again, I need to balance this and be very clear on the doctrine of giving. God expects us to give generously and liberally. God blesses givers in abundance. However, we should not be cajoled to give through cunningly devised scams that currently pervade the 21st century church. Paul told the Corinthians to give as each one purposed in his/her heart:

> *When you feel under undue pressure to give, it is not God. It is a sign of evil manipulation.*

2 Cor 9:7
So let each one give as he purposes in his heart, not grudgingly or of necessity; for God loves a cheerful giver.
Paul also warned that some preachers had come to serve their bellies only; and such still exist in the 21st century church.

When there was a need for Moses to erect structures, God caused the people to give. There was no cajoling required. In fact, Moses had to tell the people to stop giving (Exodus 36:6). Does that happen today? Do preachers ever tell people to stop giving when the Lord shows His abundant blessings over a project?

Another point to note is that whenever someone dictates an amount that must be given, such person takes the place of the Holy Spirit. The Lord has given His children a will, and thus expects free will offerings. God does not cajole His children to give. When you feel under undue pressure to give, it is not God. It is a sign of evil manipulation. God encourages you to give so that He can bless you. He however wants that action to be heart-felt. I recently had an interesting conversation with a pastor and he told me the reason he tells members of the church to dance to the front area of the building during "offering time" is to ensure that each one is compelled to give, so that the Lord can bless them. How bizarre! Here is a fundamental principle on giving - any giving that is not wilful has no weight before God. This is another major departure from apostolic order and a sore point for the church. Money takes the central position in a lot of churches, a position reserved for Jesus only.

As already mentioned, TV money manipulators are on the increase. These "TV evangelists" employ various tactics in getting people to give money into their "ministries". One question I often ask, "if the Lord has really sent such people to raise offerings through the media, why is it that the monies must be sent to one central place – the church of the fund raiser"? I would be more comfortable if the preacher said something like this: *"take the money to your local church and watch the Lord reward you"*. But it never works that way. The money must be brought within the remit of that particular preacher. That is a clear indication that something is wrong with the process. Ultimately, God is the recipient of our offerings, so it really shouldn't matter if the money is brought into church A or church B if there is no underlying manipulative scheme.

So let's get two things straight about finance in the 21st century church.
1. No one should ever indicate an amount a child of God should give in church, except in rare occurrences where the person is acting as God's prophet to a particular individual that can't hear God for some reason. Barring that exception, any outright indication of an amount that a congregation must bring to the Lord as offering is a manipulation and has nothing to do with God. Brethren, please beware.
2. The money you give to God doesn't have to be sent to a particular ministry only. God can lead you to give to any other ministry, as He desires.

These two premises are where some preachers often go wrong thus suggesting there are hidden motives to why funds are raised vehemently and through various cajoling techniques. As already stated, never feel pressurised to give God. He leads us, He doesn't force. And He doesn't value maimed offerings brought grudgingly.

While still on the subject of finance, it is important I highlight another rather sensitive topic although I will deal with it some more in chapter two. As already mentioned in this chapter, God demands free will offerings from His people. A lot of preachers teach tithes and first-fruits principles religiously even when there is no New Testament precedence to these ritualistic methods of giving to God. Many pastors continue to base their teachings on God's instructions to Israel through Malachi but completely miss God's real message to Israel on tithes. Many have thus misled the church for centuries by teaching that God demands His tithes and first fruits offerings. These are regimented sacrifices God never demanded from His church. When you realise you've been wrong for so long, the truth is always a bitter pill to swallow but we shall examine the scriptures in depth to decisively deal with this subject.

Interestingly, some pastors now know the truth on God's requirements around giving but fear telling their brethren the truth just in case regular "tithers" then decide to stop funding the church account. That takes us back to the example of Moses. If we tell people the truth, they may actually bring more than we expect, if God is indeed leading His church. Can we trust God to stir the heart of His people in the area of giving?

THE BURDEN OF TRADITION

One of God's major concerns about Israel in the Old Testament was their inflexibility and unwillingness to acquaint with His mind per time. That is the reason He often described them as "stiff-necked". So stiff were their necks that God couldn't steer them in the right direction when required. They had their agenda passed down from their ancestors so they were not willing to explore anything new God had to say. That is why He kept announcing to them that He was doing a new thing and bringing a new covenant (Isaiah 43:19, Jeremiah 31:31, Ezekiel 11;19)

Isaiah 1: 13-17 (in The Message translation):

Quit your worship charades. I can't stand your trivial religious games; monthly conferences, weekly Sabbaths, special meetings – meetings, meetings, meeting – I can't stand one more! Meetings for this, meetings for that. I hate them! You've worn me out! I'm sick of your religion, religion, religion, while you go right on sinning. When you put on your next prayer-performance, I'll be looking the other way. No matter how long or loud or often you pray, I'll not be listening. And do you know why? Because you've been tearing people to pieces, and your hands are bloody. Go home and wash up. Clean up your act. Sweep your lives clean of your evildoings so I don't have to look at them any longer. Say no to wrong. Learn to do good. Work for justice. Help the down-and-out. Stand up for the homeless. Go to bat for the defenceless.

This was addressed to Israel in pre-church era but it is still relevant today. People in church are fed up with tradition. Even more important, God is fed up too! One of the dangers of tradition is that it has the tendency to replace relationship, which robs God of His pleasure. He created man for relationship. His desire is for a relationship that emanates from the heart and mind of the man. That is why in response to the lawyer's question in Matthew 22:37, Jesus said that man should love the Lord his God with all his heart, soul and mind. This is what is weighty before God, not abiding by a set of man-made rules.

Jesus was so opposed to tradition that He kept breaking them to teach liberating truth. On one particular occasion, Jesus broke a wicked tradition by speaking with the Samaritan woman. The tradition of His day was that Jews from Judea would not speak or have any dealings with Samaritans. Jesus leveraged his genuine thirst for water to strike a life-changing conversation with this lady, and as a result, saved an entire Samaritan village. Imagine the terrible consequence of tradition if Jesus had abided by it. The woman wouldn't have been delivered from her bondage of adultery, and the village would have continued to grope in darkness. Evil tradition is dangerous and must be dismantled viciously like Jesus did.

> *Jesus didn't only come to save mankind from sin. He also came to set us free from religion.*

Jesus didn't mince words when he directly addressed the problem of tradition in Mark 7: 13

...making the word of God of no effect through your tradition which you have handed down. And many such things you do.

What is the problem with tradition in itself? When used correctly, certain traditions can have positive results. In fact, there is good tradition. According to Frank Viola's 'Re-

imagining church', apostolic tradition is what the church should actually be following:

Regrettably, the tradition of the apostles has been largely ignored today. It's been viewed as irrelevant in the eyes of many contemporary Christians. In other words, the apostolic tradition has been buried under a mountain of human tradition ....
How quickly we forget that the church belongs to God and not to us. It's part of our fallen nature to follow our own ideas regarding church practice. To enshrine our own traditions. To canonize our own personal preferences. To institutionalise what fits our own ideas of success rather than to follow what Jesus and the apostles have handed to us.

Something goes wrong with tradition when it is the tradition of men. It then becomes mere tradition, lacking the potency to save and the authenticity to continue. Men love tradition. Human beings like sets of rules that govern sustenance. That is the reason man always seeks a formula for God. Jesus deliberately defied the tradition of the Pharisees to make a statement – you can never put God in a box! This is an important truth: Jesus didn't only come to save mankind from sin. He also came to set us free from religion.

In Mark 7, we see Jesus taking a swipe at those religious bigots for their emphasis on tradition. Notice that I use 'religion' and 'tradition' interchangeably in this context. Looking at the plot again, the tradition Jesus quarrelled with was one that couldn't give life – mere tradition of men. That's the problem with religion or men's tradition. It is always outwardly focussed with no emphasis on inward renewal. Tradition places self-imposed boundaries and in most cases, opposes the move of God. So dangerous is tradition that it regularly replaces the plan of God for His church. Jesus said men were beginning to teach their traditional doctrines as though they were the commandments of God. How scary this sounds! Substituting God's absolute will for weak traditions will short-change any people from God-ordained destiny. The present day church often finds herself in this situation. Let's examine some traditions currently ripping the church of the fullness of God's life.

"SUNDAY SERVICE"

This is probably one of the oldest traditions of church and one of the most difficult to dislodge. A church meeting on a Sunday is not bad at all. It becomes a problem if that is the only time that is considered permissive. In other words, if a church group realises that another day of the week suits everyone's schedule, there should be the liberty to cancel "Sunday service". If that liberty doesn't exist because of a "mother-church" control, then it is redundant tradition that is not life-giving. Life in church must not be restricted to a Sunday morning meeting. The church has the liberty to choose a day or days that suit her.

> *We cannot be confined to Sunday as a worship day. Similarly, we can't be confined to a location as the worship centre.*

It is important to note that God does not require a Sunday morning service. The early church met daily and we too can meet daily in our days, if our schedules permit it. We cannot be confined to Sunday as a worship day. Similarly, we can't be confined to a location as the worship centre. If the church can overlook tradition and through mutual agreement choose another meeting day, they are in order and will sustain God's Life without difficulty.

CALENDAR SENTIMENTS

Time was given to man by God, so that he can have a sense of responsibility and walk wisely. A man that knows he doesn't have all of eternity to set his life in order will tend to prioritise the few days he has. That's the main essence of time – to induce wisdom. Psalm 90:12

Man has however built tradition around time. This is the reason entries into every New Year are always celebrated in style. I often joke that I'd rather be sleeping into a New Year because I know God is not sentimental about year-end or new years. It is interesting however that churches plan mega programmes around such date-centred events and tag those programmes all sort of names - "cross-over night", "watch night service". It is man-made tradition that adds no value. The sentiments attached to these occasions are unfounded and it is recommended that they are de-emphasised. Some go on to tag or label the year, all in a bid to entice people's emotions. Please understand, time is important but we are not bound by it. Wishing someone a "happy new year" is in order, just as saying "good morning". I look forward to a day the church will welcome new years without the usual pomp and festivity.

God operates by seasons. Understanding the season of one's life is more important than attending a church service on New Year eve or praying into the New Year.

TITLES

Anytime someone calls their pastor or his wife "daddy" or "mummy", I cringe and always remind them that such titles fit their natural parents only. The concept is purely cultural for most people but has now been imported into church and accepted as norm. Let me state clearly that this is not entirely bad if all parties involved are happy with it. It becomes a problem when some pastors expect or even demand to be referred to as "daddy" or "father-in-the-Lord". That then becomes a problem. Elders should be accorded double honour, as Paul admonished. Honour however is not in the titles we attach to their names or the official names we christen them. Honour is shown in relationship and speech. Therefore, leaders in church should not take offence at being addressed without titles. While on this subject, it is important I mention that a man's worth is not qualified by the title that precedes his name. The man's function and fulfilment of assignment releases value out of his life irrespective of the title he bears. So there are many bishops, reverends, apostles, evangelists who are so called on earth but do not function as such. Paul admonished Timothy to *"make full proof of your ministry"*. In other words, show your commitment to your assignment by the function, not by your title. Leadership in Christ's body is not office or title centred. Instead, it is function driven.

Take a look at Paul's opening greetings in all of his epistles. He always referred to himself as "Paul, an Apostle of Jesus Christ". Not once did he call himself "Apostle Paul". That is instructive. Paul wasn't title driven. He addressed himself based on his function. In Paul's days, the brethren would have referred to him on first name basis. How can we prove this? When the Jerusalem council of Elders met and wrote a letter to the Antioch church (in Acts 15, verses 23 to 29), the names of four Apostolic workers were mentioned – Barnabas, Paul, Judas and Silas. Not one of them was addressed as Apostle or any specific title. So simple were men in the early church that title was the least of their concerns. A church leader that considers it a dishonour to be addressed without lofty titles is out of apostolic order. Titles are men's means of feeling accomplished. They mean nothing to God and should be de-emphasised in the Body of Christ.

CHURCH MEETING STRUCTURE/SEATING

This is another sensitive piece in tradition that deserves some attention. In the early church, members gathered with no idea of what was ahead of them in a particular meeting. Church meetings were spontaneous and entirely under the leading of the Holy Spirit. The central figure was Jesus Christ only and every other person gathered around Him for worship, and to hear what the Spirit had to say to His church. There was no regimented "order of service". Hear what Paul had to say to Corinthians about that in 1 Cor 14:26:

How is it then brethren? Whenever you come together, each of you has a psalm, has a teaching, has a tongue, has a revelation, has an interpretation. Let all things be done for edification.

The Corinthian church was full of life and everyone had personal encounters with the Lord. Thus, in their meetings, people had testimonies to share of what the Lord did through them over the last few days. Each would have seen the Lord Jesus express Himself during the week, so they looked forward to recounting those personal experiences to the brethren when they gathered for church meetings. Often times too, the Lord gave them new songs that no one had heard before. He gave them prophecies. These people had real encounters with Jesus outside church such that when they gathered at church meetings to share their experiences, such gatherings were always explosive. Everyone had something to say about the Lord. Where is that in the church today? Congregants now sit passively in pews waiting to be told what the Lord is saying and how to live their lives. In interest of maintaining "order" in the house of God, only a few selected individuals now address the church and others listen. Questions are often not entertained, and in some large assemblies, you have to file out pretty fast to enable another set of congregants assemble for the next "service". This practice is entirely passive, and is a departure from God's idea of church.

> *All saints in the early church were not priests by title. They were functional priests who had access to God*

Back to the interesting Corinthian church: So passionate were these Christians that sometimes they spoke simultaneously which of course caused rowdy sessions. This is what I imagined was taking place. Brother John starts sharing his testimony of how the Lord took him to heaven and gave him a message for the Corinthian church. Sister Cornelia then remembers the Lord gave her exactly the same message albeit through a dream. In excitement, she immediately interjects to share her own experience. Just as she's speaking, she begins to prophesy and Bro Romero hears strings of sentences that are in the lyrics of a song the Lord gave him that week. In excitement, he too begins to sing the song. All of these are done with the best intentions to share the life of God in them with others. However at some point, chaos sets in and that's why Paul had to address them to exercise self control. A man's spirit is subject to him so one doesn't have to speak before another finishes. That is simple courtesy. Paul's warning however did not take away from the fact that the Spirit of God freely moved in that church. Everyone ministered to everyone. Ministry wasn't an exclusive reserve of a few "highly anointed" people. There was mutual subjection to one another. Passivity was thrown out of the window, as everyone had a strong sense of responsibility to minister to the body and express the personality of the Lord Jesus daily. Today, it is easy to talk the Christian talk in church on Sunday and live another life on other days. It was not so in the early church. They lived every day expressing the life of Jesus. Little wonder the church grew at a fast pace. Evangelism was not mere activity. Christians lived in the most attractive way that advertised the Lord's Kingdom. All saints in the early church were not priests by title. They were functional priests who had access to God in reality and expressed His mind to one another. How powerful!

The picture is different today. The church over time developed an order of service, perhaps in a bid to curb the Corinthian-style rowdy challenge. This extreme position limits the church in allowing us experience the spontaneity of the Holy Spirit. In some instances, the Holy Spirit has succeeded in bypassing the agenda of men (when He is allowed) and the results have been phenomenal. In reality, that should be a daily / weekly experience in the church.

Another interesting aspect of church is the seating arrangements. Most churches are arranged in theatre style, with a stage. Front rows are reserved for the special breed called ministers and a visitor who unknowingly sits in the front seat reserved for the pastor may be politely shown another seat in the audience. I once attended a large church meeting that was overfilled such that attendees were led to the overflow. Surprisingly, there were many seats still vacant in the main auditorium reserved for "pastors and ministers". That is the pitiful state of the 21st century church. It has become a camp of first and second class citizens under the pretext of honouring men of God. As Christ came to minister and not be ministered to, shouldn't the pastors be the ones standing while others sit? That is a question to ponder.

> *What we have now are platforms for celebrities who enjoy their moments of glory by exciting the passive crowd with what they want to hear.*

STAR PERFORMANCES

This flows from the previous point. In a theatre, the audience is always passive while the cast performs. The same mentality pervades the church. I often say that church is sometimes another expression of show-business, with each actor taking turns to entertain a passive audience. As if to confirm this theory, the congregation clap their hands when one "actor" leaves the stage even if he goes up to lead prayers or read out an announcement. The church has become so used to entertainment, that clapping for every of those acts is always instantaneous. If you are to attend a modern day church conference ("conference" or "convention" are terms used to describe unusually big church meetings), there are certain features that may stand out in the meeting. Prior to the meeting, you would most likely have received a colourful album-style poster showing the faces of the guest ministers and profiles that detail their pedigree. When the meeting starts, you will likely notice that these guest ministers are nowhere to be seen as praise and worship starts. You will notice that they are whisked in by mean-looking, FBI-styled security agents just before praise and worship session ends and they are taken straight to reserved front seats. You will likely notice a mass choir sing a "special number" just before the host minister then walks up to the stage to announce the next guest performer. He delivers a long citation on the guest minister (a common phrase used is "pastor of the fastest growing church in....." or "the man of the hour"). If God was to move the way He did in the days of Herod, many men would have died when their citations are being read (Acts 12:21-23).

The guest minister takes strides to the stage and the expectant crowd bursts into thunderous cheers and simultaneous applause in appreciation of this fine minister. You then wonder, is God truly the centre of this party and excitement? Jesus said in Rev 3:20 that He is outside while the party is on. A lot of times, we still shut Him out of our meetings.

I have not painted this picture to ridicule the church or the conferences we hold. Many of these conferences have been great blessings to the body of Christ despite their imperfections. What I am attempting to highlight in this section is that the church has ceased holding all-inclusive believers' meetings. What we have now are platforms for celebrities who enjoy their moments of glory by exciting the passive crowd with what they want to hear. Church, please wake up.

RELIGIOUS BURDENS

Matthew 11:28
Come to me, all you who labour and are heavy laden and I will give you rest. Take My yoke and learn from Me, for I am gentle and lowly in heart, and you will find rest for your souls. For My yoke is easy and My burden is light.

Jesus came to save man from religious burdens. In the passage above, we see Jesus addressing Israel and calling them out of religious burdens of the Pharisees into a lively relationship with Himself – the giver of life. He promised rest, not the forced labour we have in church today. In present day, someone's spirituality and commitment to the Lord is usually measured by how outwardly busy and generous the person is in church. I have sat in meetings where "workers" are appreciated with gifts and the outstanding ones receive recognition for increased levels of activities. Reward systems are built around how much burdens people can bear, even though these are burdens Jesus never placed on His church. The common one is seen in programme-driven churches. People are required to be in church many times in a week, and failure to turn up at these meetings is frowned at by church leadership. They are required in a departmental meeting or a church meeting, or need to attend a "mother church" conference. Please understand that fellowship cannot be forced. If people are coerced to attend many church meetings, that questions the existence of true Christian fellowship.

> *Where God's Spirit flows, there is liberty, not yokes of bondage.*

Another burden is that people are compelled to live up to a specific spiritual level, for example fast for a certain number of days compulsorily. That often tallies with the year-end sentiments, as though fasting in December is guarantee for a successful next year. Reading Isaiah 58: 6, the real essence of a fast is to carry out good works by undoing heavy burdens and setting the oppressed free. Fast should not be the burden, but the burden remover. Please note that fasting is essential in a Christian's life. So if an individual can realistically fast for a length of time, it is not a burden. Burden sets in when everyone is expected to fast for as many days as the spiritual leader.

Anyone under the burden of religion has the liberty to drop it. Where God's Spirit flows, there is liberty, not yokes of bondage. In the scripture we read above, Jesus admonished that His yoke is easy and His burden is light. In other words, He has made it easy for us to follow Him. It is same reason that John the beloved Apostle wrote *"His commandments are not burdensome"*. 1 John 5:3.

The devil paints a picture that it is difficult to serve God. Reading 2 Cor. 11:3 explains that his goal is to corrupt the believer's mind from the simplicity that is in Christ by imposing burdens Jesus already took away.

MEGA CHURCHES

In certain parts of the world, mega churches are becoming a trend. The term "mega" qualifies the size of the regular attendees on a Sunday morning. There is nothing wrong with large assemblies, not at all. When we arrive at God's throne, we can be sure to meet a mega crowd gathered to worship the Lord. John in Revelations 7:9 reported that he saw innumerable multitude worship the King of kings. So the problem is not the great number of people that gather in these churches. The concern is the level of fellowship that exists among the brethren. Are these churches as relational as Christ would want His church to be? As an example, if the pastor runs into one of the members in a shopping mall, will he recognise the member? Does a professionally run Sunday "service" substitute for depth in fellowship? Even where there is a supposed strong home fellowship network, are people's questions truly being answered? And most importantly, is

Christ central in these churches or do celebrities share the show with Him? I don't have the answers to all these questions, especially because I have not been to every single mega church. In fact, I have only been to 2 or 3. I am only throwing this topic out there as a food for thought. One thing is certain – Jesus is not assessing the performance of the church by the multitudes that gather every Sunday. His assessment yardstick can be seen in what He said about the seven churches of Asia in John's recording of Revelations.

WHERE IS JESUS?

I will close this chapter by asking this important question about the present day affairs of His church – where is Jesus? Have we allowed Him to take the central position of Lord and Decision Maker or has He been relegated to a position where He is only called upon to help in dire situations? Is He in the driving seat or would we rather play political games with His Father's business? Are the things that matter to Him the driving force of the church? Where is Jesus and what is He saying about the 21st century church?

Chapter 2

Church and Money

The subject of money is a sensitive one in the church today, and thus deserves an entire chapter devoted to it. As mentioned in chapter 1, money has caused major rifts in the church. On the other hand, it has also been put to very good use by those who know the importance of money as their servant.

Let's start with the basics. Why has there been so much gravitation towards money in these last days? If money is good, why does it appear evil on some occasions? How long will the drama around money continue?

As discussed already, money has always tried to play a dominating role since the first century church. We know of the example of Ananias and his wife whose desire for money, fuelled by the spirit of greed decided to be deceptive and play a fast game on the church. As we should know, the main problem wasn't that they kept back a portion of the money. The problem was that they were crafty about their giving and told a lie to cover up their plans. That lie to the Holy Spirit brought instant judgement. Today, the Lord still demands total honesty in the area of money but sadly, many fail Him. Let's be clear, the problem isn't just about Ananias' and Saphira's offering. The problem was their attitude towards money and God. Their understanding of God was too little neither did they fully understand the dynamics of money. Let me say it more directly, any pastor who spends church funds as he/she pleases and for personal gains is in breach too, thus keeps company with Ananias and Saphira. Taking it even deeper, any child of God who does not recognise God in how he/she spends money is also out of order. Christians are merely custodians of God's money and we will account for how we spend money at God's judgement throne.

PREACHERS AND MONEY

As an introduction, the present day disposition towards money was discussed in chapter one. At the risk of sounding mediocre, I dare to mention that money is no yardstick for fulfilment. Being a multi-millionaire should not be the goal of a Christian, never mind that that message is sunk into our minds from many prosperity preachers. Does God desire that we are rich? Yes, He does. However, He does not measure prosperity by the size of our bank accounts. True prosperity is measured by the virtue flowing out of a man.

> *True prosperity is measured by the virtue flowing out of a man.*

The number of people you have been a blessing to, and the amount of good works indicate how prosperous you are. It is as simple as that. This is the reason Abraham was judged prosperous. He is still a blessing to mankind today, according to the covenant God established with him. Jesus echoing this notion said *"beware of covetousness for a man's life does not consist in the abundance of things he possesses*" (Luke 12:15). He also said *"Do not lay up for yourselves treasures on earth, where moth and rust destroy and where thieves break in and steal; but lay up for yourselves treasures in heaven, where neither moth nor rust destroys and where thieves do not break in and steal.* (Matthew 6: 19, 20)

Jesus taught important lessons here. The earth is a temporary location. If our measurement of wealth is dependent on the world's system – stocks, bonds, real estate and other investments, then doom is inevitable. Thieves break in always, even if you live in the most secure environment. 'Thieves' can manifest in many forms including economic recession. Jesus' message was direct – earthly investments are terribly unsecure. Good works store up treasures for a man in heaven. I recently explained this in an article titled "the value of money". Money is a store of value. This attribute of money intrinsically enables it transfer value to a medium at the spender's choice. That then means that we can transfer value through good works that are registered in heaven's records permanently, if we choose to. We can also choose to transfer value to filthy lucre and earthly pleasures. The choice is ultimately the spender's. A truly prosperous man is one that God recognises as His partner in ministry because he chooses to spend money mainly for good works in God's kingdom. Such man does not see financial increase as a means to show off but sees the increase as an opportunity to be used by God in fulfilling His purpose on the earth,

One of the main problems in church about money is linked to the celebrity obsession discussed in the previous chapter. Churches now spend ridiculous amounts of money to fund events and programmes that promote the brand of the denomination and the image of the pastor, not necessarily the kingdom of God. One of the reasons pastors cultivate the culture of giving among their members is not only to propagate the gospel. Money is also being used to nurse leaders' ambitions to be known, recognised and celebrated. To balance this, it is important I state that there are still genuine servants of God who are in ministry for what they can give to God, not what they can rob off the people.

There is a teacher of God's word that I respect very much. This man lives in the middle-belt area of Nigeria and travels around the world to conduct exposition sessions. No doubt, this man is an anointed teacher, and one of the deepest expositors I have come across in my life. Something however strikes me about this brother (as he likes to call himself). Apart from the fact that he is not a title freak, his simplicity is exemplary and I have not observed him promote his image. As far as I know, he is not on any TV programme. One of the amazing things is that after his teaching sessions, this man's ministry feeds all participants that attend. And even more interesting, he raises no offering all through the seminars. He has committed himself to ministry, not egocentric campaigns prevalent among many TV preachers. I know another man in the Republic of Ireland whose ministry conducts annual prophetic conferences solely at the expense of the ministry. At these conferences, offerings are not collected and funds are never raised directly or indirectly. The purpose of the conference is to bless people, with no hidden agenda. That, to me, is real ministry. Jesus said *"freely you have received, freely give"*. I know there are many other examples of such sincere ministers of the Lord around the world whose heart desire it is to share the gifts of God with the brethren without charging a fee for it.

The typical conference setting described in previous chapter is classic example of where ministers raise ridiculous amount of money. There is a common trend of how this is done. At such conferences, an offering is usually taken earlier in the meeting. Typically, the host minister makes a call for offering. When the guest minister finishes preaching, he also raises another offering. At this juncture, people's emotions are high after hearing a moving message (it is even likely that the Holy Spirit accomplished great things in the meetings). The guest minister tells the people to "seal the blessing by sowing a seed". Where was that done in the New Testament church? Does that mean I lose my blessing if I don't sow the seed? I have heard of guest ministers who ask their hosts what the need in the church is, so as to determine the level of funds to raise at such meetings. This is the level the church has reduced herself to, and high time we cried out against such evil. Church meetings should not be focused on raising money and if Jesus is central at our meetings, we will observe He doesn't place so much emphasis on money as we do. Jesus taught on money but often did so to warn against worldliness and the potential dangerous attachment to money.

> *Jesus taught on money but often did so to warn against worldliness and the potential dangerous attachment to money.*

EMPIRE BUILDERS

The reason money continues to be a sore point is because of man's desire to dominate others. God made us dominate His creation, but any desire to dominate other men is a departure from the truth. Preachers turn to empire building techniques as a way of stamping their authorities. This is fine by the world's standards. I work in a multinational institution and I know disaffection thrives because of man's fallen drive to surpass others, display one's laurels and prove that he is better than his peers. This is fine in the world but is completely unacceptable in God's kingdom. It is for this reason Paul admonished the Philippians to esteem others better than themselves (Philippians 2:3). The world's mindset is selfish and individualistic. God's Kingdom is the exact opposite – selfless and community focused.

The faulty mindset of the fallen man is what has been transferred into church. Ministers and church leaders have now resorted to church growth techniques, not necessarily to impart the body of Christ as a whole but to build empires. Ministers want to be known above other ministers. This unchecked evil desire needs fuel to thrive – money! That is the origin of our problem. Ministers rob their church members to build these empires. They resort to all types of gimmicks, some of which were discussed in chapter one. They prioritise money and tell members to pay tithe into where they're being fed. This is used as a mechanism to trap all funds internally such that regular givers will always give God via that church alone. Let me be clear: if you belong to a church, it is ideal that you bring your offerings to that church. It is *ideal* but not *mandatory*. Never mind the present-day deductions that the "store-house" in Malachi is where you are fed. Who feeds ultimately? God! It thus means there is one storehouse – God's house. It also then means that God will receive your gifts through any house of His that is truly called by His name. Hence, any pastor that demands that the church account is the only means through which God will receive members' offering is out of order. Most times, such pastors are led by greed, not the Spirit of God. Sean Akinrele addresses this subject aptly in his book, *'Foxes in the vineyard'* :

...... it is clear that God's reference to His temple was singular, not plural.

My reservation is with the exclusive claim by pastors of believers' tithes, leaving the Christian neither discretion nor latitude in the matter. Leaders ought to rather teach followers the truth, and allow them decide whether their local church is doing enough to qualify as 'fertile ground' for all their financial devotion. My financial commitments to my local assembly should be dictated by several factors and not imposed by selective scriptural 'proof-texting' as is the current Pentecostal practice.

> **If people stop giving to their Lord, then their relationship with Him is questionable.**

I know a man who once functioned as a pastor. This man taught the members of the church that they could give God their offering through any true ministry, as they are led by the Holy Spirit. He said he owed the people the truth and told it in a balanced way. His position was to let the people know that their offerings were needed in the church they belonged but if they felt led to send it elsewhere, they were free to do so. Such bold preachers are rare in our days. It takes boldness to handle the truth and discharge it without fear of potential repercussions. Paul said something important in his second letter to the Corinthians. He said, he (and his co-apostolic workers) did not handle the word of God deceitfully but instead renounced every hidden works of darkness (2 Cor 4:2). If every leader in the 21st century church can declare the same, then church would be a much safer place. What we have today is a lot of underlying deceit motivating unrighteous actions, especially around the area of money.

Let me relay a personal experience. A few years ago, I had a strong impression in my heart that we should stop emphasising "offering time" in church but that people should still be encouraged to give God by dropping their gifts in a basket at the back of the church auditorium. I walked up to my pastor to discuss this but by some interesting coincidence; he had thought of exactly the same thing and had planned to raise it with me on the same day. With ease, we recognised this as the mind of God and went ahead to implement it immediately. Of course, this was a paradigm shift for the rest of the church and initially, a few people forgot to drop their gifts. Some had to come back to church or be reminded by friends. The church settled into the rhythm after a few weeks and thus we eliminated the undue focus on money. Neither did we operate the "tithe-card" system for close monitoring of what people gave to their God. We will discuss the tithe-card in more detail later.

The system I described above worked seamlessly and still works. However, we have received guest ministers into church and some of them are uncomfortable with it. One in particular told me that if we continue with this method, the church will always have insufficient funds because people will secretly stop giving to the Lord. That kind of talk makes me wonder what our motives are when we urge people to give. Is it to fund the church account so that there is enough to spend lavishly or is it that people can get into the culture of wilful, non-regimented giving? If people stop giving to their Lord, then their relationship with Him is questionable. Jesus taught a remarkable principle – where the treasure is, there the heart will be also (Matthew 6:21). This works vice versa too, i.e. where the heart is, the treasure will be also. So if people stop giving because money is de-emphasised in church meetings, it is an indication that we must return to the most important principle of loving the Lord. Upon that, our understanding of giving will be deepened. Saints should know the Lord to the point where they can hear when He requests that they empty their accounts. Therefore, leaders should teach people the truth that sets free from the bondage of mindless ritualistic giving.

If ministers can be broken again, the concept of Empire building will be abandoned. For as long as we continue to have unbroken vessels lead churches as shepherds, finance will continue to be a sore point for the church. If we truly can seek the Lord and have Him reveal His mind to us about money, then shall we be able to move away from the deceitfulness of material riches. Read the Lord's mind about money and riches in His address to the church at Laodicea.

Because you say 'I am rich, have become wealthy, and have need of nothing' – and do not know that you are wretched, miserable, poor, blind, and naked... Revelations 3: 17

From this bible passage, it is clear that money is not the ultimate goal where Jesus is concerned. In fact, true prosperity is only available in the Lord. On the subject of the trap in material wealth, there is an important lesson from the life of a man written by Olanike Olaleru in her biography of Reverend Akindayomi, "*The Seed in the Ground*":

At the start of the church, Reverend Akindayomi suffered such heart-rending poverty and privation that at a point it became difficult even for some of his very close aides to continue with him. They left. Yet in spite of that, the man of God was most selective of gifts of cash, cars, and even lands. His main focus was pleasing the Lord and building according to the pattern given him.

TITHE CARD

This needs to be addressed because it has become rampant in our days as another control mechanism through which some ministers manipulate the church. People often refer to Jesus' monitoring of the Treasury box in the temple to justify this practice but let's examine that particular scripture:

And He looked up and saw the rich putting their gifts into the treasury, and He saw also a certain poor widow putting in two mites. So He said, "Truly I say to you that this poor widow has put in more than all; for all these out of their abundance have put in offerings for God, but she out of her poverty put in all the livelihood that she had. Luke 21: 1-4

It is important to note that Jesus as a Man realised He had such a short time to fulfil purpose. Hence, He combined nights and days to teach everything He came to earth for. As a result, Jesus taught His disciples and others who cared to listen at the slightest opportunity. He kept teaching His Kingdom principles and found real life examples to illustrate His points almost everywhere he turned to. With that in mind, a re-examination of the widow's mite illustration will throw open two key points:

> *What does God deserve? Just 10%? Certainly not!*

1. Jesus went up to the treasury because He had an important lesson to teach. It is on record that that was the only time Jesus took this action. He wanted His followers to know His assessment criteria on giving, that giving is not in the face value of the amount given but in the sacrifice attached to it. It is as straightforward as that. Jesus knew who He would see at the treasury and decided to leverage that as a training opportunity.
2. Jesus, as Lord has the exclusive right to sit over the Treasury. The offerings we bring to God belong to Him, as God's First Born. Jesus' action also teaches that He alone as Lord can review what people give, not an appointed preacher or pastor. So, away with the tithe card as the method for monitoring people's faithfulness in giving. There is no record that the early church recorded offerings. This is a practice that slipped into the pack of many man-made ordinances

as a way of sustaining manipulations that transfer control to the pastors.

TITHES

The subject of tithe card smoothly leads us to the topic of tithes. Tithe was briefly introduced in previous chapter but we will review it critically in this chapter.

If you have been a Christian for a year or more in a 21st century church, you may have heard this phrase used : "If you don't tithe, things will be tight". I categorically state that this is not the truth but merely a famous manipulative remark. In fact, the opposite may be true. If all you give God is tithe, then things may be really tight.

To ensure we do justice to this topic, we will start from the beginning. We first heard of tithes when Abraham in pre-law era gave Melchisedec a tenth of his spoil from the battle of the kings. Abraham gave a tenth as a mark of honour for Jesus (Melchisedec was a physical manifestation of the Messiah). This was the first and only time on record that Abraham ever gave a tenth of his income to the Lord. Before that, Abraham had a lot of money, and not once was he recorded to have paid tithes. Abraham's action was to recognise God's help in the achievement, and God didn't command him to bring the tenth portion. This links in with what we discussed previously. God appreciates heart-felt offerings that flow out of man's initiative. He didn't command Abraham to bring a particular amount as offering. In the same vein, He expects you to bring what you believe He deserves. Give that some thought. What does God deserve? Just 10%? Certainly not!

Thereafter, Tithe was introduced in early Israel as a national social welfare scheme. God's plan was to ensure that widows, orphans and the poor of the land were properly looked after. God is passionate about justice and fairness. Therefore, He made provisions to ensure there was equality in the body, and to ensure no one lacked while others lavishly spent in abundance. Thus, He instituted a special welfare system in Israel that is comparable to the system He initiated in the early church. The ultimate plan was that distribution would be balanced in His family and that none of His children would lack good things that others enjoyed.

At the end of every third year you shall bring out the tithe of your produce of that year and store it up within your gates. <u>And the Levite, because he has no portion of inheritance with you, and the stranger and the fatherless and the widow who are within your gates, may come and eat and be satisfied</u>, that the Lord your God may bless you in all the work of your hand which you do
Deut 14: 28-29

And I will come near you for judgement; I will be a swift witness. Against sorcerers, against adulterers, against perjurers, <u>against those who exploit wage earners and widows and orphans, and against those who turn away an alien</u>...........will a man rob God? Yet you have robbed Me! But you say 'In what way have we robbed You?' In tithes and offerings.
Mal 3 : 5, 8

We see in these passages that God's focus for tithe was to ensure the poor never lacked. He also made ample provision for the priests through the tithes principle. In fact, we see that the context of Malachi's warning is that the poor had been neglected. Further down in chapter three God urged that there should be meat in His house, indicating that God wanted the abundance collected for onward distribution to the needy. God is not a consumer of meat and grain. God's anger against those who kept back their tithes was because of the evil intent and selfishness behind their motives. The curse is not because they didn't give God their money or income but because they truly didn't care for the poor. We need to get this right so I will repeat it. God's goal is that the poor do not suffer when there is divine supply close enough to them. He is therefore angry when the poor are neglected, even if the tithe is physically brought into the temple because His objective has been left undone. This is one of the reasons Ananias and Saphirra paid that maximum penalty. Their deception meant they were uninterested in helping the believing community wholeheartedly. People are God's passion, but often times the focus shifts from His goal into the subject of tithes in monetary terms.

In the New Testament church, there is not one record of tithes being paid. The early church in Jerusalem looked after each other by creating a communal purse. The rich and the poor had even supplies and the church functioned according to God's will. In his epistles, Paul kept encouraging the churches in Europe to share their supplies in love. He also collected offerings to help the persecuted Judea based Christians who were in dire need.

So let each one give as he purposes in his heart, not grudgingly or of necessity; for God loves a cheerful giver. 2 Cor 9: 7
Distributing to the needs of the saints, given to hospitality
Romans 12: 13

Not once was the church in any of these locations asked to set aside a specific amount or fraction of their income. Paul encouraged Christians to give as they determined in their hearts because God does not accept offerings brought grudgingly or out of necessity. He loves cheerful givers. No apostolic worker placed the burden of tithes on the churches they planted because they recognised the era of the Holy Spirit, thus the new believers were released into the liberty of a free walk with the Holy Spirit. Why then must we coerce people into a tradition of tithes and first-fruits? These are requirements that the Holy Spirit never placed on His church from inception.

Let's also examine what Jesus had to say about tithes:

Woe to you, scribes and Pharisees, hypocrites! For you pay tithe of mint and anise and cumin, and have neglected the weightier matters of the law: justice and mercy and faith. These you ought to have done, without leaving the others undone. Matthew 23:23

People who try to justify tithes in the New Testament often quote this scripture, but we should review what Jesus really meant by identifying a few salient points:

1. Jesus was addressing His disciples but talking about the Scribes and Pharisees. He was not giving His disciples a commandment neither was He teaching a kingdom principle as He would normally do, sometimes through parables. A careful study of His teachings to His disciple shows that not once did He institutionalise tithes. If anything, He promoted

sacrificial giving as a way of honouring God. 'Sacrificial' is however relative to individuals.
2. Jesus was addressing an Old Testament practice, not instituting a New Testament constitution. This is where people often misinterpret the Lord.
3. Jesus emphasised that justice, mercy and faith were the critical elements of God's Kingdom, above tithes. Justice links back to what we discussed earlier about helping the poor. So Jesus was saying "helping a blind man cross the road is more important than paying tithes of mint and cumin". Doing good, enforcing justice and mercy, and acting in faith are more important than bringing tithes.
4. Jesus also said "these you <u>should have done</u> without leaving the others undone". This is in the past. In other words, at the time you focused so much on paying your tithes, you should have shown your neighbour kindness and still brought the tithes (since this was a law in Israel). Notice he wasn't telling His church to begin to pay tithe. As in point 2 above, Jesus was addressing the era of the law when tithes was a law to Israel. I repeat that Jesus never instituted tithes. He didn't teach against it either but He clearly said it wasn't weighty enough before God. That speaks volumes.

This is the only scripture where Jesus spoke about tithes, and even at that, He addressed it in the Old Testament context. Not once did He discuss first fruits with His disciples and not once did He give it as a condition to receive God's blessing. What He simply said in Luke 6:38 is "give" and it shall come back to you. That "give" was not confined into a fixed amount or percentage as some church leaders try to teach. Jesus simply said "give", and left us with the Holy Spirit to lead every area of our lives, including our manner of giving.

Friends, if you already pay tithes, I encourage you to continue because giving in its entirety is good practice, and reveals God's nature in us. But bear in mind that "tithing" is not what God requires in this dispensation. He wants us to give obediently every time, and wants easy access to our money. Only then, can He truly bless us with financial abundance.

> *If simplicity returns to the church, perhaps our demand for people's monies will reduce.*

Why then do preachers complicate the Word of God by trying to box Christians into what God did not institute for His church? It becomes an unrighteous practice when leaders know this truth and decide to hoard it. Their emphasis on giving is often borne out of a large budget incurred on behalf of the church. A lot of churches spend so much money on buildings. Some spend a lot on image-polishing programmes and other non-kingdom related projects. All of these have to be funded by tithes and first fruit offerings, hence the clamour. This will be discussed further in chapter 4.

I have seen startling figures on how much some churches spend in our days, which clearly indicate the reason preachers cajole and coerce people to bring their hard earned money by all means. It is not because the Lord commands it. Often times, it is because their budget and pockets demand those offerings. On some occasions, some churches place a levy on all members in preparations for a specific major event. These are termed "sowing" but it is wrong to mandate people to "sow" or give a particular amount. People do not earn equal salaries, so such method of raising funds in church is unfair and unrighteous. It is permissible in social clubs but is unacceptable in church. Some churches have many poor people among them, yet the pastors and leaders live lavishly off the tithes and first fruit offerings of these helpless people. That cannot be righteous!

It is important I mention that the purpose of this chapter is not to indict all pastors. Many pastors and church leaders I know are sincere about their calling, and many sincerely teach the obsolete principles of tithes and first fruits simply because they want people to be blessed by God. Surely, not all pastors play the extortion game. Very many are honest men and women that love the Lord and desire to please Him.

If simplicity returns to the church, perhaps our demand for people's monies will reduce. If church leaders stop competing among themselves on the size of their church buildings, the category of ministers they associate with or even the size of their congregations, then there is hope that true revival will return and money will be dethroned in the heart of many. Jesus called mammon "unrighteous". The god of money is working against the plan and purposes of God. If unchecked, mammon can wreck great havoc in a man's life. If money is forcefully pushed aside from the central position it currently occupies in a lot of churches, only then can we yield to Jesus as the Bishop of our souls.

As God's child, I encourage you to transit from tradition into liberty. Beware! It is not easy stepping away from regimented offerings. God can demand for 100% of your income at any time but walking in that liberty is His ultimate aim for courting us into lively relationships with Him.

THE TRUE ROLE OF MONEY

As mentioned in chapter 1 of this book, money is only the means to an end. Wealth is not measured only in financial terms. The real wealth believers have is their relationship with God. Our real wealth lies in the covenant we have with God, not the balance in our bank accounts. The same goes for the church. The real wealth of the church is that she is married to Jesus, and that through the church, Jesus can express His mind and character on the earth. Material possessions do not define a church, as we've seen in the book of Revelations. The building a church owns is immaterial to Jesus. We shall discuss more of this in latter chapters.

How then should the church interact with money? We must rule money and defeat the spirit of greed. When Paul said he kept his body under subjection (1 Cor 9:27), he wasn't just referring to sin as that scripture is often interpreted. He meant he kept his desires for worldly pleasures under subjection and defeated ambition for possessions, which only have transient value. Paul was unequivocal in saying he took that action to prevent eternal separation from the Lord. How serious! Unchecked fleshy ambitions can ruin a man with the same venom as besetting sins. I will use a personal example to illustrate this further. Some years ago I bought a car. Shortly after that, the Lord told me in clear terms that He was bringing some money my way, but He gave a clear instruction. He said, "Don't change your car". It took a while for me to agree with this condition because of my flair for flashy cars. I finally agreed and while I still admire beautiful cars, I have not changed my car (for a few years now) in order to keep that desire for cars under subjection.

It may sound simplistic but it has weighty implications before God. As simple as it sounds, this is where some of the problems of the church lie. We have tried to be renowned thus we spend a lot of money in portraying our image to the world. The early church didn't need money to portray their image. In fact, at a point Peter said "silver and gold I have not" (Acts 3:6), yet notable miracles took place around him daily. Money was not the key driver in the first century church. The Lord played a central role and money worked as a servant. That is the position we should return to; a position where we can command money and not be subject to its enticing influence.

Here then is the crux of the matter. God will cause money to bow to the church when His church focuses on what matters the most – establishing His covenant. The Lord said *"seek ye first the Kingdom of God ....."* (Matthew 6:33). That is instructive. Buildings, programmes, and other financially demanding projects need to be de-emphasised. Seek the Kingdom and real money will come into His church. I agree with people that teach believers how to create wealth and manage it. It is good to learn wealth creation principles but the starting point for dominating money and making the best use of it is to prune our motives and centre them around God alone. No fame, no popularity campaigns on Television, no trying to get the attention of the world, no show-off of new buildings and new private jets. Just focus on Kingdom building and the church will be rich enough to establish God's covenant on the earth. Contrary to most popular opinions, the church doesn't need all the money in the world to make impact. The church doesn't have to be the richest group (in monetary terms). We simply need as much money as the Lord releases, when we tailor our priorities on what He desires. I learnt an important lesson from my mentor, which I will share on this forum. If money was the most important means through which the church would make impact, God would have ensured the richest man on the earth is a Christian. That is not the case today. The richest people on earth are not necessarily believers. This is something to ponder.

I re-state here that money has an important role to play in ministry but is not king. Instead, its role is that of a servant. Jesus expects that we are faithful with money (spending judiciously on kingdom projects), so that He can commit true riches to the church. True riches are however measured by how His covenant is established on the earth through His church. The wealth of the church is the amount of spiritual power we command; and blessings that transcend generations are true riches. Note that Abraham was already "rich" in cattle and other material possessions. He had a retinue of servants. By the world's standard, Abraham was already stupendously wealthy. Yet, God looked at this "poor" man and swore that "In Blessing I will bless you, in multiplying, I will multiply you". The blessing Abraham received that day was spiritual and has now run through thousands of generations. That is wealth in its true sense. There is a similar lesson in Job.

Also, his possessions were seven thousand sheep, three thousand camels, five hundred yoke of oxen, five hundred female donkeys, and a very large household, so that this man was the greatest of all the people of the East.......Then the Lord said to satan, "have you considered My servant Job, that there is none like him on the earth, a blameless and upright man, one who fears God and shuns evil?"
Job 1: 3 & 8

There is something interesting about what God said of Job when He boasted about him to satan. God mentioned nothing about his wealth and greatness on the earth. He was the wealthiest man in the East yet the Almighty God ignored that fact about him. He simply boasted about Job's true wealth – God's nature in Him. God's joy was that He looked into Job's heart and saw Himself. He showed off to the devil about Job, yet He didn't mention anything about his material possessions. Job's real wealth was God's covenant with him, not the balance in his bank account.

Just as we saw in Abraham and Job, Isaac was also distinguished by the covenant God established with him. Even more interesting is the fact that God promised his half brother, Ishmael a lot of money. He said Ishmael would control a gigantic financial empire yet reserved the covenant of eternal life for Isaac.

Thus says the Lord: "Let not the wise man glory in his wisdom, let not the mighty man glory in his might, nor let the rich man glory in his riches; but let him who glories glory in this, that he understands and knows Me, that I am the Lord exercising loving-kindness, judgement and righteousness in the earth, for in these I delight," says the Lord. Jeremiah 9:23-24

We see again that knowing God and being established in covenant with Him is true wealth, and that should be our confidence as believers.

Friends, these examples are instructive. God is not impressed with money and the church's material possessions. The private jets, the multiple streams of incomes, the large church buildings etc do not mean anything to Him, and are not the indication that God is increasing the church. Unbelievers (symbolised by Ishmael) enjoy these blessings too. The indicator of real wealth is in how much of His Life we transmit to mankind.

As I close this chapter, I once again will attempt to balance the message. Poverty is a curse. The Lord has not designed that His people should live in poverty. We must have abundance of funds to do His will, which He faithfully supplies. There is no need to devise extortion scams to fund church projects. If God commissioned the project, He will fund it. Let me state categorically that the church needs to move away from spending heavily on material things that do not focus on establishing God's covenant. A good example is church buildings. It is disheartening that so many churches are in huge financial debts in their efforts to own buildings. Buildings have no eternal value and should not gulp a major part of the church's budget. God used buildings in the Old Testament to paint a picture of what was to come – the invisible building of His church. Now, according to Peter "You are lively stones being built up as a spiritual house" (1 Pet 2: 5). The church is a spiritual house! It is therefore surprising that some churches rent or buy buildings, and even "dedicate" them as Solomon did under the old covenant. This practice has no New Testament precedence, just as building was never priority for the 1st century church.

It makes financial sense to own a building, rather than rent, especially where monthly mortgage repayments and rents are almost equal. That makes sense. But the main point here is that buildings are so inconsequential that they should not define the church's budget. Given that it is not my responsibility to define the percentage that should be allocated to rent, the church's leadership should take the required responsibility and ensure funds are spent to improve human life and preach the good news of salvation. Most of church's money should be spent on people, not on material things. The opposite of that takes place in most churches today.

If the church can return to the simplicity that characterised the first century church, financial sanity will be restored in church. If church leaders can collectively decide that money is a servant and not lord, then perhaps their approach to money will change drastically. If preachers and church leaders can humbly decide that the time has come to live normal lives, be simple and spend in moderation, then perhaps the church will be truly broken once again and repent for the sins of the past. If we all can make the commitments Paul made and declare that "we keep our bodies (and fleshy demands) under subjection", then the church's true wealth will be restored and we will once again walk in power, which includes financial liberation. That journey can start today.

Chapter 3

What is wrong with Clergy?

Contrary to what the world dictates, that a system produces seemingly excellent results is not good reason to retain it. "Never change the winning team" or "never change the winning formula" are common statements in the world today. Thus, it is increasingly becoming difficult to argue with "success", as defined by worldly standards.

However, in the church, results need vetting through spiritual lenses and success should never be measured by mere facts and figures. For example, that a church has grown to a sizeable number of regular attendees on a Sunday morning is not a measure of the church's depth and love for the Lord. Neither is it a measure of spiritual quality. In worldly business organisations, success is determined by figures. Some churches borrow marketing principles from the world and grow membership through well researched and proven psychological means. This equates to employing Babylonian

Church is ONE family by divine design. Setting aside a sub-family within this important family is unscriptural.

principles in Zion, a combination that is always destined for disaster.

The basic problem with official clergy is that the concept has no scriptural precedence. We examined this briefly in chapter one but this subject needs further review. Church is ONE family by divine design. Setting aside a sub-family within this important family is unscriptural. Over the years, I have observed that the moment I am introduced to anyone as a 'pastor', I am treated differently. The expectations of me change and I am often assigned certain privileges that "ordinary" Christians don't enjoy. This is the norm in church today and I challenge that notion in very strong terms. Church is a spiritual house. Church is family and there is only ONE FATHER over this family. Jesus Christ is the First Born, and the rest of us are brothers and sisters in this big family. At a Bible study meeting in church some years ago, I raised the issue of equality. I told the brethren that every single Christian is equal but this didn't go down well with a number of people. Some disagreed and insinuated that there is no such equality in the body. I dare say that many of our practices in church today are functions of inherited notions and traditions, not products of personal convictions from walking with the Lord. Let us examine what the scripture says about equality of the brethren:

You also, as living stones, are being built up a spiritual house, a holy priesthood, to offer up spiritual sacrifices acceptable to God through Jesus Christ 1 Pet 2: 5

For Whom He foreknew, He also predestined to be conformed to the *image of His son, that He might be the <u>firstborn among many brethren</u>* Rom 8:29

Then Peter opened his mouth and said "In truth I perceive that <u>God shows no partiality</u>. Acts 10:34

For both He who sanctifies and those who are being sanctified are all of one, for which reason <u>He is not ashamed to call them brethren</u>. Hebrew 2:11

It is clear beyond doubt that God's preferred system of government is direct rule. As mentioned in chapter 1, this is the reason He was disappointed when Israel rejected that system of government. God always desired direct relationship with man. He would come into the Garden of Eden to fellowship with Adam and interact with Him. He created man for one-to-one relationship. Further down the line, we saw Him visit Abraham and discuss affairs of surrounding nations with this mere mortal. God wasn't bored in heaven but He loves man so much and has always desired true close fellowship with man. Little wonder then that David, standing in awe asked Him *"what is man that you are mindful of him, and what is man that You visit him?"* (Psalm 8:4).

Man was always in God's thought but the fall of Adam resulted in a great gulf between divinity and humanity. For a period of approximately 4000 years, God employed a temporary indirect rule system until the gap between Him and man could be permanently bridged. Often times, people refer to the leadership of Moses and Joshua to support the single pastor clergy system but that is incorrect. These patriarchs were a type of the Christ, and thus a shadow of things to come, until the Messiah Himself arrived on the scene. That is why the writer of the book of Hebrews opened by saying God who once spoke to us by His prophets has now spoken to mankind through His Son (Hebrews 1:1-2). His message had been consistent all along through His servants, the prophets but He summed it all up in Christ. So Moses, Joshua, David and compatriots are not enough reason to enforce a single-pastor clergy system on the church. These men were God's stop-gap measures until Christ arrived and restored His original relationship with man. If that is clear enough, we can take it a bit further. Now that God's objective has been met, man as a priest, has direct access to Him through His Son, Jesus - the High Priest. No man therefore must take the position of the High Priest in church today.

It is clear that the clergy/laity segregation prevalent in the 21st century church is a departure from God's truth and purpose for His church. The problem is not that there are leaders but that these men and women are officially designated as being separate from the rest of the church. Any attempt to tamper with God's design is transgression. We see that in old temple constructions supervised by Moses, God gave specific instructions on measurements. That shows His heartbeat towards His house. Man should therefore not impose a segregated clergy system. It robs God of His pleasure and robs the church of the benefits in God's fullness. How did the clergy originate?

Frank Viola dealt with this in his book, *Pagan Christianity*:

Up until the second century, the church had no official leadership. That it had leaders is without dispute. But leadership was unofficial in the sense that there were no religious "offices" or sociological slots to fill. New Testament scholarship makes this abundantly clear. They were religious groups without priest, temple, or sacrifice. The Christians themselves led the church under Christ's direct headship. Leaders were organic, untitled, and were recognised by their service and spiritual maturity rather than by title or an office.....

Ignatius of Antioch (35 – 107) was instrumental in this shift. He was the first figure in church history to take a step down the slippery slope toward a single leader in the church. We can trace the origin of the contemporary pastor and church hierarchy to him. Ignatius elevated one of the elders in each church above all others. The elevated elder was now called the bishop. .....

According to Ignatius, the bishop had ultimate power and should be obeyed absolutely......

At the time of Ignatius, the one-bishop rule had not caught on in other regions. But by the mid-second century, this model was firm established in most churches. By the end of the third century, it prevailed everywhere.

A special class called clergy did not exist in the newly born 1st century church. As soon as the church was established, the Apostles took initiative to tend God's sheep because of their spiritual maturity, having spent many years with the Lord Himself. They therefore presented the church with the truth and offered spiritual guidance. Peter in particular received instructions directly from the Lord before He departed, so he had a sense of responsibility to tend and feed the church. Therefore, elders and leaders in church should exist. We see this pattern in scripture as mentioned already. The Apostles took over as elders and nurtured the body by feeding her with God's truth. A key role of elders is to preserve the body from wolves and false doctrines. The Apostles filled the role very well but notice that they didn't constitute a fraternity of any type, neither were they segregated as a special class within the church. These men were subject to the body, the same people they stepped up to lead. This is the reason Paul could look Peter in the face to correct his faults (Galatians 2:11).

Sean Akinrele's *Foxes in the Vineyard* also addressed this topic of segregation:

There is therefore no scriptural basis for the modern division of the church into 'Clergy and Laity'. As we saw earlier this was a development of the 2nd century when a professional class of Christian ministers was introduced much like our modern trade unions and professional associations to protect the special needs of its members.
As a result, the believer's personal service to God as a priest and minister of the Gospel is de-emphasised and rather monetised. Today the popular refrain from our pulpits is 'bring all the tithes'. The implication is: as long as I pay my tithes and other financial commitments to my leader's ministry, I am absolved from any major personal involvement in Christian ministry and evangelism. My pastor and other 'full-time' workers are doing so on my behalf. This is most unbiblical.

For emphasis, I state that the early church knew no official clergy. Everyone was hungry for the Lord and everyone enjoyed direct access to God. There was no need to call Peter to pray for a new home or John to "bless" a new vehicle. Instead, when Peter was helplessly incarcerated by Herod, the church rose to pray for him. Every man functioned as a priest to the Lord, and this is what the church should be today. Creating an atmosphere that segregates some "superstars" is not right and must be challenged rigorously. It is direct transgression against God's plan, albeit some unwittingly commit this transgression. It is important to mention that while we continue to maintain our equality in Christ, there are different levels of grace and anointing. Some people have walked deeper with the Lord, and know Him more than others. Clearly, our experiences in the Lord are not equal but our rights in Him are.

ORDINATION

A common practice in the institutional church is that men and women are selected from the multitude (laity) and "ordained" into a "ministerial service". They are usually given a title to differentiate them and often times their sitting positions change in the church. In some orthodox settings, even their dressing change and they are made to perform roles that "ordinary" members are not permitted to perform. They are often called "ministers" and that ordination is usually seen as a mark of graduation to higher things in the Lord. In fact, from close observation, it has become a reward mechanism that some churches have adopted into their systems. This has no scriptural basis. This important ceremony has caused some rifts in the body yet it continues to be the climax of many believers' spiritual experiences. Ordination is usually used as a mark of confirmation on the person's calling.

Do not neglect the gift that is in you; which was given to you by prophecy with the laying of the hands of the eldership. 1 Tim 4: 14

Many things are wrong with the system of ordination as we have it in church today:

1. In the example we see above, Paul tells Timothy that by the laying of hands of the Elders, certain gifts had been imparted unto him. That is divine truth. God transfers spiritual gifts through the laying of hands by the carrier of the gifts. However, Timothy, the young apostolic worker was not brought into a special class by that action. Gifts were deposited into him for the work of the ministry but that action didn't separate him into an exclusive fraternity reserved for a select few. It is important to get that right. We should continue to lay hands on people so that there can be transference of power and impartation of spiritual gifts but this does not require elaborate ceremonies if the objective is right.
2. "Ordination" is not a New Testament trend. Hands were laid to transfer gifts, not commission people into "ministry". And those who received these gifts went on to use them extensively to the glory of God. An example is the appointment of deacons to "serve tables" (Acts 6:5). These men were not commissioned into a special class. They served the body and provided great support to the apostolic workers. This was all about team work. They were appointed to serve, a role they performed wholeheartedly as servant-leaders. Leadership is important. What the church needs is functional leadership that is based on Christ's leadership principle of humility. This, He taught and displayed when He washed His disciples feet, even as their Leader.

3. Even after elders and apostolic workers had hands laid on them, they remained subject to the body of believers which they had been called to serve and stayed accountable. It is for this reason Paul reeled out his private experiences in letters to the churches. He told them of his personal challenges and areas of struggles. That he was an apostolic worker didn't imply that he couldn't be subject to the body. The body functions by mutual subjection, not through a servant-master practice prevalent in the clergy/laity settings.

Therefore, setting aside a special class called clergy has no justification in scripture and has no basis to continue.

SALARIES

If we maintain that the clergy concept was foreign to the 1st century church, how then can the 21st century church justify the segregation that currently exists? Moreover how can we justify paying salaries to pastors and other "full-time" clergy officers? What exactly is full-time ministry? The latter question will be tackled in this chapter. As we discussed when we looked at the subject of tithes, God made a provision for the Levites in the old dispensation because He had commanded that they should own no possessions in the inherited land. The Lord promised to look after them and offered Himself as their inheritance (Joshua 13:33). To keep His promise to this special tribe of priests, He commanded that lands be available for them to dwell in but they were not to inherit the land like other tribes did. This is a peculiarity with priests. They are different from the crowd and are not attached to material possessions. As for the Levites, ample provision was made for them through the tithes and offerings of Israel (Deut 14:29).

In current dispensation, no such requirement is made. The body of Christ is now a family of priests. As it has been mentioned severally in this book, there is no other visible special class of priests in Christ's body. We are all kings and priests unto the Lord (Revelations 1:6).

How was clergy salary introduced into church? This problem started sometime in the third century.

In the third century, Cyprian of Carthage was the first Christian writer to mention the practice of financially supporting the clergy. He argues that just as the Levites were supported by the tithe, so the Christian clergy should be supported by the tithe. But this is misguided thinking. Today, the Levitical system has been abolished. We are all priests now. So if a priest demands a tithe, then all Christians should tithe to one another!
Culled from Frank Viola's Pagan Christianity

A paid clergy system is not scriptural. All pastors and "full-time" clergy should get a vocation. Get a job or run a business. Feel the rigour and challenges of a normal life and through that process communicate the good news of God in corporate and business circles. Paul combined his tent-making trade with apostolic assignments. Even though Peter and his business partners didn't return to their fishing business as a main source of income, there is no record that they received regular salaries from the church. Yes, the church would have risen to help them during times of need. Their trips would have been willingly funded by church. One thing remains clear – they never treated apostolic work as a vocation. This is where the 21st century church may have taken the wrong step. Today, people are trained to be pastors by attending formal institutions. Not only has clergy been carved out as a special class in the Christian church, it has also been designed as a vocation. So you may hear little boys say "when I grow up, I want to be a priest". Some pastors transit from "secular" jobs into "full-time" ministry. These notions are foreign to the 1st century church.

There are some instances where it is impossible for Christians to combine regular jobs with the ministry of the Lord. A perfect example is that of missionaries. In such exceptions, the church should take the financial responsibility of taking care of the needs of such itinerant ministers because they realistically cannot sustain office jobs if they have to keep travelling to spread God's Word. But if a person has not received a call from the Lord to quit secular employment, he or she should continue to labour in His vineyard through regular engagements with the world in corporate circles. Governments and the business world are mission fields that also need to be won unto the Lord.

Let us examine the background. The institutional facade around church sometimes compels her to conform to the style of the surrounding world. The world is a field of institutional players - from companies to schools; from army to the police; from governments to social clubs. The world is tightly structured and extremely institutionalised. Having observed this seemingly good trait in the world, the church is aligning to the world by creating institutions. In most churches, you find a one-man leadership system. That pastor then oversees a board who in turn oversee the rest of the church. Even more interesting is the succession system of such institutional churches. The sole pastor's wife is usually the deputy leader and often times, other family members are brought onboard to ensure there is smooth succession when the leader passes on. Most times, church is just another family business empire. Purely worldly! But that is the dynamics of institutions. There must always be humanly devised continuity and effective leadership succession.

To sustain institutions places heavy demands on finance which takes us back to the vicious cycle of the dependence on money. In addition, sustaining the world's style of institutions requires a major demand on human resources, which again links in with the dependence on money for salaries. Perhaps if we return as a church to the simplicity of organic church as it was in the 1st century, our demand for money will reduce. If we dismantle our institutional structures and keep church truly organic, then we may need less employees to run ministry 'professionally'. The world runs successful and professional organisations but the church is not in competition with the world. If anything, we should be that example of simplicity.

As in previous chapters, I will balance this. The church should not compromise excellence for simplicity. Instead, simplicity should bring out the excellence in us. The crux of the message here is that we do not need to build complex organisational structures behind our churches in order to be considered effective in the community. As we see in first century church, the simpler the better. And despite their simplicity, the Lord added new converts daily to the church. The Holy Spirit is the one that breathes on our simplicity to inspire excellence and transmit His life to the dying world. We do not need to tie in so much unneeded financial and human resources just to maintain popular denominational brand names. It is interesting that some churches even advertise on billboards and electronic mass media. Such use of money is questionable, and is proof that the power of God is lacking in those churches. While there may be nothing wrong with advertisements, the concern here is on the motives driving them. Are we truly advertising God's Kingdom through those adverts or men's empires? Simplicity precedes results and kingdom results announce themselves to the world.

> *Every true child of God is a full-time minister. God hasn't called us into part-time service.*

Let us return to the simplicity exemplified by the first century church. I challenge pastors who currently receive salaries from church to stop it, pick up vocations and live normal lives. Being a pastor does not separate you from the rest of the church. If you are not paying your church members for attending church every Sunday morning, you have no scriptural reason to continue to receive salaries. This is not the easiest step to take in one's life but it is worth it. May the Lord have mercy on us, especially in areas where we unknowingly failed to follow His plan for His church.

WHAT IS FULL-TIME MINISTRY?

I grew up as a Christian hearing this term – full-time ministry. It is still being used today to even further segregate the church. So broadly speaking, there are three main groups in an average 21st century church – laity, part-time clergy and full-time clergy. In order of hierarchy, the latter group is often seen as the most senior. It consists of people who have taken 'bold steps' to abandon their day jobs and in 'faith' step into another source of income. Often times, these people testify that it wasn't initially easy but after some years, their persistence paid off. I then wonder what faith is required to merely change one's source of income. In fact, most times, this new source provides a lot more supplies for the full-time pastor. But even beyond that, I challenge the full-time ministry notion in its entirety because it has no scriptural basis for existence.

Every true child of God is a full-time minister. God hasn't called us into part-time service, neither does He expect we give him partial attention in our lives. If that is true, then it negates the idea that some people are called to "serve" in the temple as Levites did. That is not a requirement in the New Testament church. Priestly services are now being done by all children of God and we need no special category of priests to perform any roles for us. While some claim to receive the calling into full-time ministry, it is interesting to note that the financial reward for such people is enormous. There are pastors who receive salaries from their church, and because their wives are on the ministerial board, they are also paid monthly salaries.

In addition to both salaries, the church may pay for all their expenses – rent, utility bills, transport etc. Such way of life is not only greed-induced, it is callous! And what irresponsible way to spend church fund! Such pastors and their families are invariably living off the tithes and offerings of the congregations, some of whom are not even as financially comfortable as the pastors. It then calls to question the motive of the 'call' into 'full-time ministry', and greatly shows that injustice is rife in the 21st century church. Is this how Christ designed His body to function? Certainly not! If a pastor is practically enriching himself with church funds, is it a surprise then that such a pastor will be livid if church members decide to pay their 'tithes' in another church?

For emphasis, I maintain that full-time ministry as it is generally presented in 21st century church is scripturally baseless. Every child of God is a full-time minister, not just those who quit their secular jobs to work in a church office. I therefore state that except acting on the express instruction of the Lord, pastors and church leaders should remain in secular employment. It is not sinful to do so. They should conceive business ideas and run kingdom style businesses. Stop the salaries, except in cases where the funds are used to support Christian workers that genuinely cannot work. Avoidable salaries rip church of the money she should be using to serve the poor and spread the good news.

HONORARIUM

This is another sensitive area where the 'clergy' has missed the mark by great miles. Let's examine the scripture that is usually quoted to support honorarium in the 21st century church:

Let him who is taught the word share in all good things with him who teaches. Gal 6:6

What was Paul really saying in this context? Clearly, he wasn't institutionalising a church practice. He made a recommendation, not a New Testament law that teachers of the word must be honoured with good things. "Good things" places the initiative within the remit of the person communicating it. In other words, the giver decides what to give. Today, ministers expect to be given huge cash gifts when they visit a church and failure to do so will incur wrath of most ministers. In fact, if you want to ensure a minister never visits your congregation again, invite him or her over to preach and do not give any gifts at the end of the preaching sessions. Honorarium is not only expected. In some cases, it is demanded. There are ministers who send contracts to churches when they are invited to preach. The contract stipulates advance fees and the amount they expect to collect after they preach. It then makes of no importance the Master's direct instruction – "*freely have you received, freely you should give*". If we are directly or indirectly charging people for the gospel, then we are departing from His instruction. A minister that grumbles or fumes because he received no cash gifts when he honours a preaching engagement has departed from the faith. Harsh as that may sound, it is reality. No church owes any preacher gifts. Paul only made a recommendation, a good one at that. However because this particular one suits our selfish desire for money, we often teach it as a commandment. It becomes an unwritten law in the 21st century assembly and churches are under pressure to 'honour' guest ministers even when they do not have the means to do so. The danger here then is that a church that is not financially buoyant can get starved of the teaching gifts in the body simply because the church cannot afford a 'decent honorarium'. This is evil and must be checked.

I once belonged to a church that was struggling with huge financial debt. As a result of this burden, members had to sacrificially give to sustain the church through her difficult period. The leadership also took a wise decision to drastically cut down expenses by cancelling all programs for the year; this meant telling all invited preachers that the church's financial difficulty was the reason for cancelling scheduled events. Only one invited guest still offered to visit the church to be a blessing at his own expense. Only one! He was willing to give without having anything to gain materially. It causes Jesus pain when we trade the gifts He bestowed on us for money and other material benefits.

One of my teachers in School of Ministry once narrated a story to the class. He told us of a "man of God" who visited another church on invitation to preach. The host minister then stood on the podium and read this guest minister's citation in the usual flattery manner practised in most parts of the church today. As the citation was being read, the Holy Spirit whispered clearly to this guest minister and asked him a question *"Did I send you here, or did the honorarium send you?"* It is best imagined how that guest minister would have ministered God's word under such conviction. This is the reality of our days and preachers need to question their motives for honouring preaching invitations. Is it to be known, celebrated and given handsome financial rewards? Or is it to be genuine blessings to God's church? If it is the latter, then I challenge preachers to start refusing honoraria, especially when they visit fairly small churches and can sense the financial burden these churches bear to raise cash gifts.

When Balak hired Balaam to curse the children of Israel, the latter initially refused at God's instruction. However, deep within Balaam, he lacked spiritual depth and was greedy for material gains. So he kept asking God if he should honour Balak's invitation until the Lord consented conditionally. A man who feared the Lord would have listened the first time. David said *"once the Lord spoke, twice have I heard"*. (Psalm 62:11). God need not repeat Himself if you heard Him the first time. His will remains His will, and as we later found out in same chapter of Numbers 23, God said He never changes His will. What happened here is that Balaam hoped God would change his mind and permit his visit to Balak simply because he was attracted by the honorarium Balak had offered. Balaam was ruined by greed. This is still the case today. Some preachers visit a city or country, arrange tours of preaching engagements and collect honoraria from church to church. The reality is that some of these preachers embark on fund raising exercises through these preaching engagements. Often times God's gifts in them are being merchandised and that breaks God's heart.

This has made me compare preachers of our days to the prophets of old. An example is Jeremiah. Given the kind of messages he preached, honorarium would have been far from his listeners' minds. He was revolutionary in approach and his message though being the truth was not accepted by the nation or their successive kings. In fact, instead of honorarium he received prison terms. At a point he was left to rot in a dungeon for speaking the truth.

Then Jeremiah left Topheth, where God had sent him to preach the sermon, and took his stand in the court of God's Temple and said to the people, "This is the Message from God-of-the-Angel-Armies to you: 'warning! Danger! I'm bringing down on this city and all the surrounding towns the doom that I have pronounced. They're set in their ways and won't budge. They refuse to do a thing I say."
(Jer 19: 14 – 15 Message)

This passage raises some questions. Among his listeners, who would have given Jeremiah honorarium for declaring woes as God's message? If present day preachers are declaring God's truth, will they really be in popular demand? Are we playing to the gallery rather than fearlessly declaring the truth like Jeremiah did? Can we handle the rejection or would we prefer compromise to sustain the flow of invitations and the honoraria such preaching engagements deliver? These are just questions to ponder.

I know a preacher in the city I live who shared his personal experience with me. Over a period of time, he received invitations to preach in various cities across Europe. As is the practice, he would normally receive a "brown envelope" after every preaching engagement. On one particular occasion, the church he visited didn't give him any monetary gift after preaching and deep within his heart, he was hurt. The Lord then told him that honorarium was beginning to take a hold of his heart which called for instant repentance. From that day, when he visits a church, he receives the honorarium and gives it back to the same church as his gift to them. This was his own way of defeating the spirit of greed that was beginning to grip his heart. May the Lord grant us the courage to take bold corrective steps in our attitudes towards money. Amen.

> *Every church leader should build bridges across denominations and sincerely wish the body well.*

Again, I will attempt to balance this. It is good and strongly recommended to give to elders and teachers of God's word. It is the honourable thing to do, especially as some may be in need for various reasons. Honorarium should however not be subtly demanded or institutionalised. It should not be taught as a law. But where a church can afford to give, such kind gifts to God's servants will always be rewarded by the Lord.

CLERGY RIVALRY

Another evil that has eaten deep into the body of Christ today is the severe division between certain ranks of the clergy. The rancour and bickering I have observed between these men of God is disheartening. As discussed in chapter 2, one of the major problems is the subtle competitions between these preachers. Some want to be seen as closely associating with popular world renowned preachers and will spend as much money available to invite such ministers. Often times, such major meetings will be widely publicised to prove to other ministers that they (the conference hosts) belong to a peculiar league of preachers. I know that sounds like unfounded argument but anyone that has carefully observed church practice over the years would agree. In retaliation, the competing preachers would then organise their own versions and either invite the same popular preacher or align with another Pentecostal icon. These conferences are expensive to organise and explain why the church always places demand on people to keep giving more money. If there was no rivalry and no point to prove to "ministry rivals", churches would spend less on programs.

A few years ago, I was invited to have lunch with a group of pastors in a European city. These pastors lived in that city and called the lunch meeting to discuss a collective concern they had. Their churches were located in the same area and another well established church in that city was at the verge of relocating her meeting venue to this neighbourhood. The relocating church is well known in the city and has a sizeable membership, so these pastors felt threatened by the move into their neighbourhood. Their main concern was that they could lose members to this well known brand hence the lunch was called to devise a collective checkmating strategy.

As we ate, I listened to their plans and kept thinking to myself that this can't be right. Certainly, it is anti-kingdom practice. In hindsight, perhaps I should have spoken the truth at this meeting but these were men I barely knew so I reserved my comments on that occasion. I wasn't on the original invited guests' list but was invited at the last minute by a friend. I believe the Lord allowed me into that meeting to see the degradation of the 21st century church. Friends, when people hold meetings to checkmate another church, it is indication that the original focus of these people was not to build the kingdom. It is clear indication that brand name is more important than seeing souls genuinely saved. If a pastor is threatened that he will lose members to another church, then the 21st century church has real problems to sort out. Shouldn't the work of a church complement the work of another church in the same city? The answer is simple and known to every true believer.

I once had to represent my pastor at a pastors' meeting and someone made a passing comment. He said a particular church had started a radio station. Almost instantaneously, another pastor suggested that our denomination could start a radio station too. How ridiculous can this needless competition become? If any action was necessary, wouldn't it have made more sense to partner with the church that already obtained a radio licence and agree to use slots in their station, rather than spend money on a new radio licence?

If we continue to compete with one another, the commonality of our parenthood as saints then comes into question. Every church leader should build bridges across denominations and sincerely wish the body well. If one member suffers, we all suffer. If one rejoices, we all rejoice. This is what gladdens the Father's heart.

PAUL AND BARNABAS

I once heard that the story of these gentlemen is what some pastors capitalise on when they compete or split ways. There are some key points to note about what looked like division between these two wonderful apostolic workers:

1. By nature, Barnabas was a soft and trusting man. When the body of believers in Jerusalem didn't trust the conversion of Paul, he was the one that invited Paul to come along and partner with him in ministry. He always gave people a chance to perform. By nature, he permitted second chances.
2. In contrast, Paul comes across as a no-nonsense stickler for discipline. He was assertive in nature and demanded top performance from associates.
3. Given their difference in nature, they had differing principles too. So in Acts 15, Barnabas took a stand that John Mark should be given a second chance to accompany them on apostolic field trips. On the other hand, Paul disagreed sharply because he didn't want an uncommitted member in the team. The difference in opinion led to a sharp contention. However these men split ways based on principles, not bitterness. Bitterness would have hindered their progress in ministry.
4. Another key factor to note is that their separation was not God's perfect will, thus not a perfect example for the church to follow. The Holy Spirit called them out in Acts 13 for a specific assignment. If the Holy Spirit didn't split them, contention shouldn't have. This then

means that the separation of Paul and Barnabas is not a perfect example for the 21st century church.

'RESPECTING THE ANOINTING'

This is a phrase I have heard countless times. The complete sentence is "you cannot attract the anointing you don't respect". An intelligent person must have crafted this and many preachers are now fond of saying it to the people they lead. I dare say that respect is never demanded, it is earned. That one is designated a pastor or a bishop is not what attracts respect. It is the exemplary life of such a person that determines the respect he or she commands. Also, that one is anointed by God is no reason to demand unusual attention or respect. If the anointing is truly present, signs will follow such a person and people will be blessed but it is still not a condition for respect. Character is what attracts respect, not just the anointing. Paul admonished the church in Corinth to imitate him as he imitated Christ. In other words, Paul was asking the church to learn Christ's traits in him. Paul was showing off the character of Jesus and that is what is important for church leaders. Church leaders who are true examples of Christ will naturally command respect.

CONTROL

There is a thin line between influence and control, thus church leaders need to exercise restraint when tending God's flock. Influence transits into control when leaders dictate to the flock specific details of how to live their individual lives. As mentioned in chapter 1, some leaders even take the place of the Holy Spirit by telling people how much money to give

God. In the past, some leaders have dictated to members of the church on what career to choose, who to marry, and so on. Many have taken the issue of accountability beyond limits, pushing it into tightly controlled relationships. This is the reason people are asked to declare their incomes so that their 'tithes' can be calculated by the church and monitored closely. Control is dangerous and inhibits the flow of God's life in the body. A pastor or elder in church should never become a figure in church such that anything he says is final. It is a terrible position to assume and has consequences.

I remember growing up as a Christian in Nigeria. There was a particular denomination that I liked very much for their sound holiness-centred doctrine. I didn't belong to this church but I would normally attend their crusades as a teenager and listen to recorded messages from the church. In retrospect however, there was a practice they adopted that I now disagree with. Any couple dating each other were not allowed to visit themselves unaccompanied until after marriage. The couple always had to be accompanied by a witness for all meetings during courtship. Failure to adhere with this requirement could result in termination of the relationship by the church leadership. This system was put in place to prevent pre-marital sex and the sincerity of the church leadership in trying to curb sin is appreciated. However, if two Christians cannot stop themselves from pre-marital sex, do they really love the Lord deeply? If they sin, shouldn't that question their spiritual maturity and preparedness for marriage? The focus should be on developing members to a point where they can overcome temptations when there is no human witness. Christians should genuinely be accountable to God and if conviction is missing in a Christian's life, something is fundamentally wrong.

Another system of control prevalent in many Pentecostal institutions is that brothers need permission from their pastors before making marriage proposals to sisters in church. I have been told that the motive of this practice is to enable the pastor curb excesses of certain unserious Christians who make dating rounds for the fun of it. Is this then the way to address the issue? There are many complex marriage situations because people have learnt to pretend in church by complying with such rules. Laws do not set free. Only true relationship with Jesus sets people free. Hence a pastor should have no control over the decision of two consenting adults. His role is to teach them God's truth and watch them mature in their walk with the Lord. If these fundamental principles are in place, the life of the church will be spiritually orderly and there will be no need for humanly devised controls.

I have a young friend that I mentor in the way of the Lord. This lady has had bad experiences with relationships so in my earlier dealings with her, I became somewhat protective. When she told me she was dating a man with questionable character, I told her to break the relationship, and didn't mince words on that instruction. Then another man came into her life and she told me about it. This man didn't appear to have any relationship with the Lord. My initial reaction was to dictate a reasonable action but it occurred to me that I was beginning to control this young lady's life unknowingly albeit with the best intentions. So I decided to handle the situation differently. I told her that having gone through a series of bible study together, she now had God's word in her and that through His Spirit in her, she knew the right action to take. I also firmly told her that I would go with any decision she took. This gave her a sense of responsibility and accountability to God and she took the action I expected regarding that relationship.

We can so easily transit from mentoring and leading into controlling people. Control is evil and must be checked promptly. When Jesus asked Peter to take an active role of shepherd over His flock, He used two key words – "feed" and "tend". None of these translate into "control".

SUBMISSION

A key feature of the clergy system is that a special category of leaders carved out from the believing community often assume autonomy over the church. Their decision is usually final and oftentimes, in a sole pastor setting, the pastor can't be questioned. This poses great risks to the body of Christ today. I have often imagined standing in a massive church auditorium and announcing to the congregation that their general overseer made a doctrinal mistake. I could easily be stoned if I did that. The reason is that clergy has been presented as flawless. For fear of "disrespecting the anointing" and for fear of being labelled, people have held back their questions and concerns. Many sit in pews completely dissatisfied but dare

> *Many sit in pews completely dissatisfied but dare not challenge the "anointed of God".*

not challenge the "anointed of God". Pastors who know little of God's plans for His church then run riot over God's people as wolves and cannot be questioned by the people they lead. It is important we collectively address this as a church. Every church leader must be subject to the church. Christian service is defined by mutual subjection. If a leader makes a mistake, then those who are spiritual in church should correct him in meekness, as Paul recommended to the Galatian church. The pastor or elder even when spiritually mature is human and will err. If the erring gets away with it all the time without being held accountable by the church, it could lead to a major catastrophe.

Paul and Peter present us a good example of subjection. Peter as an apostle was regarded as the most senior among his peers of Apostles. He was one of the closest to the Lord Jesus and at point of departure, Jesus particularly charged him to lead the flock. On the contrary, Paul was initially little known. After an unusual encounter with the Lord, he began an explosive ministry to the gentiles. In the course of ministry, Peter and Paul met in Antioch and related very well until Peter made a costly mistake (which he is allowed to make, being human). Paul respected Peter but didn't overlook that error. Paul in his account to the Galatians said he withstood Peter face-to-face and pointed out his faults to him. What a bold step! This was only possible because Peter was subject to Paul as a brother. Is that common in the 21st century church? As a reader of this book, can you correct your pastor? If not, it is indication that something is wrong.

As usual, I will give this the required balance. As we discussed in chapter 1, elders are worthy of double honour in our speech to them and general conduct towards them. They should be treated respectfully but if they err, they should be corrected in love. It is safe to do so, because it serves the interest of the elders and the entire church. The key thing in correction is not to act in rebellion. Your heart must not be lifted in pride to correct your leader even when you think you are right. As Paul said, implement correction in a meek manner, not in arrogance. A leader can be corrected openly if he errs openly. He can also be corrected in secret. An important element of correction is the motive driving the correction – it must always be done to restore the person back onto the right path, and shouldn't be an attempt to prove a point or demoralise the individual.

> *You must treat the entire body of Christ with respect and cause no harm on them.*

...*Do not touch My anointed ones, and do My prophets no harm* 1 Chronicles 16:22

Oftentimes, people quote this scripture as a reason for not challenging a wrong act by their church leaders. Review the background of that scripture. God's jealous protection was over the entire nation of Israel, not just a special class. In same vein, the believing community in the 21st century church is God's anointed, not the clergy. **You** must treat the entire body of Christ with respect and cause no harm on them. The determinant of that is judged by the motive of one's heart.

As I conclude this chapter, it is important I state once again that there are many in the clergy today who are in the institution for the right reasons. Not every clergy member is after material gain. Not everyone is particular about branding the image of their denominations. Many truly love the Lord and are serving Him as they know how to. The problem however is that the foundation of official clergy as it is defined in 21st Church is faulty; and being sincerely wrong is not an excuse to perpetrate a system God did not institute. Let me be clear friends. Functional leadership in church must continue to be expressed through ministry functions and responsibilities placed by Jesus on Apostles, Prophets, Teachers, Evangelists and Pastors. Even though the whole Body is subject to the Headship of Christ, the church still needs earthly Leaders that are not officially segregated from the rest of the Body.

If we challenge the status quo, it may inspire hope that we can once again align ourselves with God's eternal plan for His church.

Chapter 4

Monuments or Church?

And He said to them "It is written, 'My house shall be called a house of prayer', but you have made it a 'den of thieves'"
Matthew 21:13

The closest resemblance to what Jesus was about to birth was the physical temple, so He referred to it as His "house", simply as a reflection of what was to come. The posture of His heart to this house is however interesting. Jesus in very strong terms condemned the activities prevalent in the temple. Religious men had taken over the affairs of the temple, and used temple worship as opportunity for intensive trade transactions. Thus they made money at the expense of the people. Rather than feed hungry souls with God's laws in the temple, they concentrated on profit bearing ventures and this attracted Jesus' wrath. He was visibly angry and didn't mince words when he described their action as being equal to what thieves did. The temple was built for prayers and Torah study, not for business deals. In same vein, the church Jesus established is being built for prayers, relationship and worship, not as a source of income to religious folks.

As already mentioned, the danger of religion is its outward focus. The inner parts remain in darkness while the outward parts flourish. This is what Jesus addressed when he drove the merchants away. These men carried out their transactions as mere activities in the temple, without paying attention to the real reason the temple was built. It is the trap of religion, and such merchandise still prevails in our churches today. Pastors and leaders spend a lot of time and efforts building brand names for their denominations and in doing so, erect structures that keep people busy. Our churches are a lot bigger but in general, lives are not changing at the same speed as our numerical growth. When that happens, religion is on the driving seat! People then think they impress God by being busy in these man-made structures but rather than give life, religion drains people of every measure of life they already have. I recently had a conversation with a colleague at work who told me that as a child she believed in God but was repelled off as she grew because God was always presented in the mould of religion! That is the problem with the 21st century church. People are being presented with religion, not relationship. The strong evidence that religion is eating deep into the church is that church leaders now raise monuments in place of church. That is the subject of discourse in this chapter.

We shall briefly examine the monument Saul raised.

So when Samuel rose early in the morning to meet Saul, it was told Samuel, saying "Saul went to Carmel, and indeed, he set up a monument for himself; and he has gone on around, passed by, and gone down to Gilgal."
1 Samuel 15:12

Why did Saul raise a monument? There could be several reasons but we shall examine a few below:

1. **Pride:** Saul could relatively be considered an achiever. Effortlessly, God delivered to him the people of Amalek. The Amalekites are the people Moses battled with immediately after the red sea crossing. Prior to Saul's reign, Israel always had one enemy or the other, ranging from the Midianites to the Amonites. In these hostilities, God would raise judges to rescue Israel. Kings that succeeded Saul also battled enemy after enemy and opposition was always stiff for the nation. Saul, however, didn't recognise he was a product of God's grace but perhaps attributed his achievements to his military acumen. Although success had been given to Saul on a platter of gold, he didn't acknowledge God as his source. I recently listened to a pastor give a detailed analysis on how pride was the main source of Saul's rejection by God. He wreaked havoc on himself and blew away a chance of being one of God's dependable generals in his generation. Saul's refusal to kill Agag wasn't only an act of disobedience to God's express instruction, the disobedience was fuelled by pride. Agag and his livestock were spared as Saul's war booties to show off his war achievements. That was the final straw for this erring king. He then had to build a monument for himself. He set a parade from Carmel to Gilgal to proudly show off that he captured a king. Notice here that the monument wasn't for God. It was to celebrate a man - Saul. That was a major departure from the practice of the patriarchs who always erected altars to honour God and remind themselves of His covenant. Hard as this may sound, many of the 'ministries' available

today have been centred around sole leaders in those respective ministries and churches. Some of them may truly have started with the intention of honouring God but allowed flesh to hijack God's ultimate plan along the journey. A lot of times, the problem starts with unchecked pride – a severely destructive sin. Pride always precedes disobedience, not vice versa. Lucifer fell as a result of pride. Being very familiar with pride, He enticed Eve with it by suggesting man's equality with God as a good enough reason to eat the forbidden fruit. When pride had fully taken hold of Eve, it was easy for disobedience to operate in the garden of Eden. May we receive grace to always search our hearts for pride that may be lurking around the corner, waiting to devour us. May we also not put on the deceptive cloak of false humility, which often tries to cover pride in a man's heart. Instead, may we truly submit to God and to one another in Christ's body.

2. **Self-esteem:** Another reason for the monument was Saul's weak self esteem. Saul's character was revealed to us in the way he treated the sacrifice of God when Israel prepared for battle. He was more interested in public acceptance than honouring Gods ordinance. We see this again when the words of women caused a permanent hatred in his heart for David (1 Sam 18:7-8). Saul suffered greatly from low self esteem. Thus the monument was a cover-up plan to hide his weakness. The celebration all around town was to show the world that he too could attain great heights in life. Saul was reacting to his low esteem. So bad was his self esteem that he couldn't handle a subordinate (David)

being praised more than him. Similarly, many ministers and preachers today are suffering from the same symptom of low self esteem. Many are threatened by the ministry gifts of those in their care. Self esteem is the reason pastors give themselves impressive official titles. Many are concerned about how they are perceived in society, so they go all out to project the image that can be accepted and liked. Some even employ brand management consultants who train them on public presentation. In short, Church leaders are now celebrities. Many crave for public recognition simply because of low self esteem.

3. **Recognition:** this was another of Saul's problems. When he brought back Agag, he lied to Samuel and said "I" have done what the Lord commanded. When Samuel challenged him over the bleating of the livestock, he immediately provided an excuse – "they" (the people) brought them back (1 Sam 15:13-15). Low self-esteem is the reason people want to take credit for success and pass on responsibility for failure to others. Saul wanted to be recognised as an obedient servant of God yet was unwilling to pay the price. We treated this briefly in chapter 1. Today, there are many pastors and leaders drawing attention to self. They do this by building massive monuments that cannot be ignored by those in society. The main objective is the recognition that comes with erecting the monuments. Jesus is often used as the excuse for these monuments but the mode of operation within some churches indicate that they are no different from what Saul built – monuments! Men are still working tirelessly in

building monuments for self, to satisfy the fallen desire for recognition.

In his book, *Church Shift*, Sunday Adelaja tackled the issue of monuments in a way that aptly captures the message I am trying to convey in this chapter:

Having met with billionaires and famous people, I have found it actually easier to approach many of them than it is to approach some pastors. God help us! Sometimes our eyes slip from the kingdom and fall onto ourselves. When our focus is not on finding our promised land and changing our society from right where we are, we start using kingdom resources to build our own kingdoms. We become egocentric.

Monuments usually manifest in many ways but we shall examine a few of the common methods prevalent in the 21st century church.

STRUCTURE

This was discussed briefly in chapter 3. In the church Jesus established, simplicity is the rule of the game. The Kingdom of God is not hierarchical in structure. That needs emphasis – the Kingdom of God does not function by complex hierarchy! It is a flat structure. Jesus, as the Apostle and High Priest of our sainthood dwells in the Father and Spirit as One. The three dwell in one accord. In same vein, God's ultimate plan is that all saints will express the same unity on the earth by fusing into one body. So the end-state model is One God (Father, Son, Spirit) and One Body (the church of Christ). What then does that mean? The structure of the Kingdom is such that the

Body is directly accountable to God. God never outsourced the responsibility of Lord and Advocate for His church to any other person. Even though the twelve Apostles will sit as judges of the twelve kingdoms during the millennial reign of Christ, the church will always remain directly accountable to Christ first and foremost.

Where does this place the gigantic organisational structures we have come to build around church? In a traditional church setting, the structure is such that the pastors of the various branches all 'report' into the General Overseer resident in the 'mother church'.

In this rather impressive organisational structure, one man sits on top of the ladder as general overseer. Others climb the ladder through lobbying, loyalty (to senior members on the ladder) and other crafty means. The basic problem with structure is that even though Christ is confessed as Lord, in reality, He does not take a central position. The man on top of the ladder often has the final say and is hardly ever challenged. What he says is final and if you don't agree with him in principle you are made to feel as a rebel or shown the door out. This is not to castigate or cast aspersions on the body of Christ. Far from it! Instead, the aim is to point out the areas where the body is ill and needs treatment. Can a General Overseer be wrong? Of course, yes! But often times, many General Overseers cannot be told by members of the church when they are wrong. The reason is because of the complex organisational structures we build in church today. The structures create a huge gulf between 'ordinary' members of the church and the top echelon. Friends, this is not the mind of

God. The 1st century church was largely unstructured and Christ freely expressed Himself in their midst. Could there be a possibility that we are stifling that expression of Life in our church meetings through these structures? I must mention again that many gifts are lying dormant in our churches because of structure. The pastor (since he is head of his own territory) preaches almost every Sunday except when he is out of town, in which case his wife is asked to preach. Whether or not this pastor has teaching gifts really doesn't matter in the structure. Others with latent spiritual gifts are made to sit passively in pews and the church is robbed of God's gifts to His body. This is injustice to Christ's body, but that is the problem with organisational structure. Structure is not always fair.

To maintain a top-notch flawless structure requires money. Thus churches deploy significant portions of their budgets into branding and marketing activities. Multimedia adverts and Billboards are used extensively to sell their brands, no different from secular organisations do. Some years ago, I flew into a European city for holiday with my family. The night we arrived, I watched an advert on TV from a church in that city announcing the visit of a popular bishop from the United States. As I watched, I couldn't help but see the flaunting of a polished brand, although I played it down and still attended the advertised program. When I arrived at the church, I honestly couldn't understand why the event was advertised on TV. Judging by the capacity of the halls, the church wasn't prepared to host the number of Christians in that city. However, to project a brand, the program was widely advertised. I arrived at the venue of the event one hour before the scheduled start time yet I had to join a long queue outside the hall. Tickets were printed to filter entrance into the main auditorium and there was a lot of agitation arising from the crowd that had gathered. At that point, I realised a lot of us (including myself) had gathered to watch a man perform at a 'show' under the guise of 'church program'. At least, that's how it felt.

> *Any true heir of God's Kingdom thinks of the body's health, not the growth of a denomination.*

On the issue of branding, I often ask myself if expensive adverts on mass media channels; image building schemes etc are judicious ways of spending God's money. Branding is expensive and needless for the church, especially because it is always focused on denominational brands thus revealing even clearer the cracks and division in the body.

One of the effects of denominational monuments is that sects are formed out of them. People reason and make decisions along denominational lines. It is ridiculous! Sectarianism is sinful and destructive, and must not be allowed to exist in Christ's body. A structure that deliberately shuts any group of people out of church is evil and is an anti-Christ structure. Anyone that has sincerely accepted Christ is a legitimate member of the Kingdom and must be accepted into the fold, regardless of the denomination they claim to belong. Anything short of that is indicative of cult practice.

Sometime ago, I attended a denominational meeting and one of the leaders stood up to address us. He said categorically that our inaction was responsible for the growth of other denominations in the country and that if we took appropriate actions, other denominations really didn't stand a chance. This man wasn't joking. I sat in total shock and disbelief. Such mindset among Christians is dangerous. It is cult oriented, not kingdom focused; and that is the effect of a rigid church structure. It puts people in compartmentalised boxes and makes people think competition within the body. I have heard pastors make comments like "we are different"; "we are taking the lead" and other such remarks that indicate the competitiveness of church structures. The church of the living God is simple in style and any true heir of God's Kingdom thinks of the body's health, not the growth of a denomination.

I will share another personal experience that highlights a problem with the "structure" mindset. 'Global Day of Prayer' is an annual event held on Pentecost Sunday in many countries of the world. It is such a wonderful opportunity for Christians to ignore denominational barriers and hold hands in praying for the church and our nations. In Ireland, my church family has participated over the last few years. I once tried to extend invitations to other pastors within our denomination but before I did that, I mentioned it to the central administrating team of the denomination. To my dismay, I received a stern warning that I wasn't permitted to do so because this was not a denominational program. Clearly, that does not portray Kingdom mindedness but that is the problem with structure. Denominational branding often supersedes overall kingdom interests.

Let me state clearly that organisational structure is not what the church needs. If we allow the Lord flow through us as He desires, the church will accomplish phenomenal heights without rigid man-made structures. The church must express organic life, and not try to imitate the organisational structures of the institutions in the surrounding world. So institutionalised have our minds become that a church does not feel complete without a brand logo, a governing board, an organisational chart, board of trustees and other elements of worldly institutions. In fact many ministries have taken structure overboard by naming the ministries by the founder's name. So it is now common to hear names like 'John Famous Ministries', named after the sole pastor who functions as head of the governing board. In such ministries, it is not out of place to find that succession plan is in favour of the wife or son of the founder. The structural framework is all about political games and schemes, which are foreign to the first century church. Peter could easily have announced the birth of 'Peter & Andrew Ministry' after Jesus departed. John and James could have set up a similar structure to rival them. But what do we see? A people bound themselves together and committed to the church that Christ Himself established. Not once did we see precedence of instituted man-made structures within the early church network.

BUILDINGS

Church buildings have become major representation of monuments in the 21st century. The first century church grew rapidly in homes but today church seems incomplete without monumental buildings. Are buildings important to God? The answer is straightforward. Does church building expansion equate to church growth and maturity? Again the answer is clearly "No". What then has led many to focus on church buildings as if that's what matters most in the kingdom? Clearly, there is strong attachment of present day believers to their edifices. Perhaps many think they can't function properly as Christians if they don't meet regularly in well furnished buildings. So many churches spend significant portions of people's tithes and offerings on buildings. I like the way Frank Viola discusses the issue of buildings in his book *Pagan Christianity*.

> *The church building played no significant role in the 1st century church*

Many contemporary Christians have a love affair with brick and mortar. The edifice complex is so ingrained in our thinking that if a group of believers begin to meet together, their first thoughts are toward securing a building. For how can a group of Christians rightfully claim to be a church without a building? (so the thinking goes). The "church" building is so connected with the idea of church that we unconsciously equate the two. Just listen to the vocabulary of the average Christian today:
"wow, honey, did you see that beautiful church we just passed?"
"My goodness! That is the largest church I have ever seen! ....

Interesting as this may seem, the church building played no significant role in the 1st century church. Instead the idea of building is well rooted in religious order of Judaism. That is why it takes me by surprise when Christians decide to "dedicate" their "temple", quite similar to what King Solomon did many years before Christianity. Temple dedication has no New Testament precedence. In fact, the New Testament church had no need of physical temples. The reason the Apostles visited temples was to preach to Jews who were yet to convert to Christianity. Church meetings held in homes and Christian Life was organic, independent of buildings. Whenever there was need to hold large meetings beyond the capacity of homes, the church would meet in a city hall for such meetings especially when the city received visits from apostolic workers who had a message for the church in that particular city. This certainly needs emphasis. The first century church thrived without edifices all over town, leaving us an example to follow. God's building is the church – the souls of men. That has been His priority and He has not changed His mind. If we continue to place major emphasis on how beautiful our buildings are, we may miss God's purpose for his end-time church.

I am not advocating that the church should begin to meet in ramshackle structures before we can please God. Neither am I suggesting that the 1st century house church style is the only acceptable mode of church in the 21st century. My point here is that emphasis in church should be on people, not the building in which they meet.

Friends, I dare say that if you belong to any church where there is undue focus on what the building and internal aesthetics look like, that could be clear indication that something is fundamentally wrong. If special building pledges and offerings are always being requested, and if the pastor refers to the building as "the Lord's house", then you can be almost sure that that building has become a monument, even when this is done with the best intentions. When asked to give repeatedly to a church building project, please always ask yourself if buildings constitute God's priority for the 21st century church.

TV PROGRAMMES

Another form of monuments is the stronghold of media programmes that men have developed over time. It is important I mention that I have been blessed by many Christian TV and radio programmes. I remember the years I lived in London. I would normally leave my radio set permanently tuned to 'Premier Radio'. The early morning bible based teachings from this gospel station blessed me greatly beyond what I can explain. I know that there are many such God-ordained media programmes which God is using to impart lives across the globe. However, when there are genuine products, fake equivalents always exist. Without meaning to pry into political affairs in this book, I will mention an example that still rings in my mind. When the United States of America was about to launch military attacks on Iraq in 2003, a Christian TV station aired a program where prayers were being requested for the US Army to succeed. This is a TV station with global coverage! How was an Iraqi Christian supposed to feel when watching such a politically motivated "Christian" event on TV?

The main problem with Christian domination of the media is that not everyone has been given a mandate by God to speak through the mass media. A lot have taken the initiative simply on their quest for fame. You only need to listen to some preachers speak on TV to realise they don't have a message that needs media coverage yet they want to be heard. It is a status symbol among co-preachers to be able to say "our church is on television and radio". I must state something categorically: The desire to be seen, heard and noticed is of the fleshy nature. As stated in previous chapters, any desire to be famous, recognised and accorded celebrity status didn't originate from Christ. The examples we see of Jesus indicate that He would rather get His job done silently. Naturally, He was famous because His good words announced Him but not once did He crave fame or public acceptance.

As already stated, not all Christian media programmes are monuments but quite a lot fall into that category. If as a pastor, you know you have no business being on TV, I encourage you to take the bold step of discontinuing such expensive needless programs. Besides buildings, mass media is another avenue that gulps the funds within a church. Churches run up debts to be able to fund these monuments and often times, the motive is simply to polish the public image of the sole pastor. To support that allegation, here is an important observation. Most of the TV or radio programmes always project the image of the leader as being on the driving seat. Other preachers within the ministry will hardly get any 'air time' because the objective is selfish! Even in cases where the 'pulpit is shared' with other teachers in that ministry, only the videos that feature the sole leader (or spouse) are selectively beamed on TV. This is the case most of the time, which presents us with the easy method for identifying monuments. Monuments are always centred on self, while the true life-giving ministries are centred on Christ.

Evangelism is one good reason ministers give for going into mass media. I agree that many TV based evangelistic programmes have produced such great soul-winning results in the past and will continue to do so. That applies to true ministries only. Monuments that use evangelism as excuse to spend so much money do not generate kingdom oriented results. One question I ask, do unbelievers really watch Christian TV channels? If we truly want to reach the dying world through the media, we need Holy Spirit-inspired ideas on how to meet the world with a language they can understand. Monuments can't deliver that expected solution. Only God can.

COVERING AND NETWORKS

"Who is your covering?" is a common question among pastors. Some present it in another way, "what stable do you drink from?" If I am asked that question today, my answer will be 'God'! We have been made to believe human coverings are needed to succeed as God's ministers but I see no precedence of that in scripture. I have mentors and leaders that I hold dear to heart but my covering is solely God. That needs further clarification. God will always place you under tutelage and functional mentorship, no doubt. He puts teachers and mentors over us so that grace and gifts can be transferred and multiplied in His church. He expects us to learn from one another and yet be subject to each other. Mentoring when used appropriately is excellent and certainly expresses God's plan for His church. Things go wrong when people, under the spirit of control, hijack that plan by placing themselves as human "coverings" to other men. God is our covering! The only time "covering" was used in the bible in human terms was in the context of marriage, simply because marriage is a symbol of our relationship with the Lord Jesus. So in reality, a man provides covering for his wife to the extent which Christ has already covered him in that home, which then means Christ is covering to both man and wife but God instituted man as head in the interest of order.

> *That you respect, admire and even learn from an anointed leader does not make that leader your covering.*

Why then have famous ministers turned "covering" into a doctrine? It is because the networks these men have developed for themselves constitute monuments. "Covering" is just another tool for control. The bigger the network, the more influence and control the preacher has around the world. Less famous ministers then proudly associate with the famous ones by boasting of the "stable" they drink from. This is outright falsehood that has no scriptural precedence. Every true church has God's life and a pastor/leader does not need to "drink" from a "stable" to effectively lead or minister. This does not negate the need for mentoring, certainly not. If you are a church leader, you need mentors to succeed. You are accountable to them and can receive spiritual gifts through your association with them. This, however, does not make them your covering! Only One person has that ultimate role – the Almighty God! So much has this false doctrine eaten deep into the body that the "covers" almost directly demand for monthly financial contributions from their "sons and daughters". They teach it as a doctrine and make those contributions a condition for sustained covering. Some even refer to the people they provide cover to as "my flock" or "my children". A lot of times, the "covering" is provided through strong denominational strongholds. So a strong "mother church" structure is implemented to ensure that the mother church monitors every single activity of the "child church". Finance is remitted to the mother church and a certain percentage is sometimes reserved for the "covering" who sits on top of the denominational ladder. Is this in apostolic order? Certainly not! Men have simply devised ways to enrich themselves, build monuments, create influence and live at the expense of others. The less famous preachers fall victim of this plot because of their innate desires to also build similar monuments at the appropriate time. So they decide to serve a "stable" to enable them build their own networks. Such networks are monuments and often times have nothing to do with God. Frank Viola treats this issue of covering in his book *'who is your covering?':*

The NT criteria for role models is always functional, not formal. While we should value the service of those who lay their lives down for us, it is a grave mistake to mark them off formally from the rest of the believing community. (This is where the "covering" teaching goes wrong!) Indeed, the honour that a believer receives from the church is always merited. It is never demanded or asserted. Those who are truly spiritual do not claim to have spiritual authority over others. Nor do they boast about their spiritual labour and maturity. In fact, people who make such claims reveal their immaturity!

As already stated, covering is only provided by God. Men cannot offer any sort of coverings. That you respect, admire and even learn from an anointed leader does not make that leader your covering. He is only an instrument of righteousness through which God chose to bless and increase you. Let this be very clear friends. If you are under a human "covering", here is a litmus test to check whether or not this "covering" is being done as a means of control: challenge the notion of covering with this leader and request for a scriptural reason as to why it exists. You know something is wrong when you are not permitted to freely challenge or express your sincere opinions. Such an atmosphere is control-driven, the essential element of monuments.

CONFERENCES

Certain types of conferences are organised perhaps with the sincere motives of blessing the body, which is great initiative. Conferences turn into monuments when like media monuments, they project the image of the convener and spouse. Conferences take the monument posture when finance is a major motivation with a central position. In most cases, because of the glamour attached, these conferences cost a lot of money thus there is financial pressure that induces a major focus on money. As Such, "offering time" becomes one of the most sensitive moments during such conferences.

As I mentioned already, there are conferences being organised by some without undue focus on money. If this becomes a church-wide practice, we may begin to dismantle the monuments of conference.

In summary, monuments do not glorify God. As in the time of Saul, monuments are ego boosting machineries created through man's intelligence. A fundamental difference between monument and church is that the former is man's innovation, the latter is being built by God.

For we are God's fellow workers; you are God's field, you are God's building. 1 Cor 3: 9

Chapter 5

The Bride and Groom

And I also say to you that you are Peter, and on this rock I will build My church, and the gates of Hades shall not prevail against it.
Matthew 16:18

Our focus in this chapter is to revisit the divine principles about the church Jesus promised to build - a process He started upon his departure approximately 2010 years ago. As mentioned in closing lines of the previous chapter, Jesus is the Master Builder of His church. Believers are the building but also function as co-labourers with Jesus. This is the reason Jesus asked that we pray for the Lord of the harvest to send labourers into His harvest. Notice in Matt 11:28, He asked that we cease from our labours. This is to enable us transfer God given energies into His labour, not ours. There is a fundamental difference between both. Our labours represent religion, His labour is Kingdom work. The difference is like that of day and night, so there should be no confusion between the two. As we discussed already, religion drains man and adds no value to him, whatsoever. Kingdom work is done through grace and delivers value to mankind. The church of the living God has been delivered from religion into a walk of liberty with the Lord Jesus Christ.

We shall examine some characteristics which distinguish the church from worldly institutions. At this juncture, it is important to mention that the church is not a mere institution. The church is constituted through Spiritual Life, a Masterpiece building of the Most High God. The church does not struggle to be visible like worldly institutions. She simply establishes Jesus' reign on the earth by shining His light in the world and through that act, the church cannot be ignored.

UNITY

Unity is a non-negotiable trait of the church which Jesus is building. The true church of the Lord is one! This is not forced unity. It is not superficial, neither does it stem from feigned peace. Love is in the DNA of the church, and with love, unity is inevitable. Listen to the heartbeat of Jesus as He prayed for His church:

That they all be one, as You, Father, are in Me, and I in You; that they also may be one in us, that the world may believe that You sent Me.
John 17:21

One way to tell a true child of God in current dispensation is the person's approach to the subject of unity. Children of God do not work against what their Father is building. Instead, as co-labourers with the Master Builder, they join Him in building His church. Let me state categorically that anyone working on dividing the church of the Lord has no place in Him. True believers emphasise unity and work towards attaining it. They think mainly of the strength of the universal church, not the prominence of their denomination.

Let us learn a lesson from Korah's rebellion against Moses.

And he spoke to the congregation, saying, "Depart now from the tents of these wicked men! Touch nothing of theirs, lest you be consumed in their sins" Num 16:26

Korah and associates rebelled against Moses and their action would have caused division in the camp. (Let reader note that Israel is representation of contemporary church). Apart from God being angry with the rebellion, He was also displeased with the resultant effect on the kindred spirit within the camp. This was why He told Moses to separate Korah and friends from the camp of Israel for a penalty. In the same vein, anyone who tries to divide Christ's body steps out of God's covering, in preparation for His judgement. Please note also that Christ's body is indivisible. When His body hung dead on the tree, the soldiers didn't break His bones. That action didn't happen ordinarily – it was fulfilment of prophecy. Not just that, it was instructive of the unity that would ensue in His body upon His departure from the earth. Let it be clear then that anyone who tries to divide an indivisible Body is on a futile mission and turns into an enemy of Jesus Christ. Like Korah, the person separates from the commonwealth of the church and steps outside God's covering. This is why Paul addressed division when he wrote about the disorder at the Lord's table in the Corinthian church (1 Cor 11).

Paul wasn't only addressing the manner in which they ate the Lord's body unworthily as gluttons. He was addressing the underlying problem of disunity which led to such indecent behaviours at the Lord's Table. A divided mindset is the reason some were sickly and even died in the Corinthian church, Paul said. Jesus is passionate about the Unity of the church He died to save. He once said that those who are not gathering with Him in unity are scattering the sheep. No doubt He is against such people unless they repent and align with Him by "gathering". Let us examine another scripture:

Behold, how good and pleasant it is for brethren to dwell together in unity! .... For there, the Lord commanded <u>the</u> blessing – Live forevermore. Ps 133 : 1, 3b

Unity provokes God's blessings. Notice that the psalmist didn't say God commands "a blessing". He said God commands "<u>the</u> blessing", which is ever flowing life. The best we can receive from God corporately is that His Life should freely flow among us as believers, which only happens when we are united. What greater blessing can we ask than this? Salvation of the unsaved will be a more regular occurrence because of the limitless flow of God's life when saints gather in unity. If we are struggling to gather fruits into eternal life, it is perhaps an indication that we need to strengthen the bonds between us. The cords that bind us are many times stronger than man-made denominations which tend to divide. In fact, our bond in the spirit is stronger than natural family ties. This is what Jesus meant in this scripture:

For whoever does the will of My Father in heaven is My brother and sister and mother Matthew 12:50

His message here was direct. Spiritual lineage is superior to natural family ties. It shows how seriously Jesus takes His spiritual family called church. His desire is that we would maintain the unity He, the Father and Holy Spirit enjoy. The three dwell together as community, in perfect harmony. Three

Persons yet in one accord, no one trying to usurp authority but instead each One exalting the other. That needs further explanation: The Father committed all judgement into the Hands of the Son (John 5:22). He also highly exalted the Son above all names (Phil 2:9). The Son always gave the glory to the Father and was obedient to Him (Phil 2:8). The Son placed the church under the leading of the Holy Spirit (John 16:13). The Three Persons function as one and mutually exalt each other. There is no competition between them for superiority. Instead there is perfect agreement in this Union. That is the same union Jesus died for the church to attain. Anything short of that level of unity is a departure from what the Lord purposed for His church. His desire is that we will be ONE church.

> *Jesus Christ is the rallying central figure in church.*

Watchman Nee discussed unity in his book, *The Normal Christian Life*:

God does not blame me for being an individual, but for my individualism. His greatest problem is not the outward divisions and denominations that divide His church but our own individualistic hearts.........

The life of Christ in me will gravitate to the life of Christ in others. I can no longer take an individual line. Jealousy will go. Competition will go. Private work will go. My interests, my ambitions, my preferences, all will go. It will no longer matter which of us does the work. All that will matter will be that the Body grows.

From my observation, one of the main causes of division in the body today is difference in doctrine. Sincere Christians sometimes find themselves drawing lines of division over issues they have strong convictions about. I dare say here that the Lord didn't ask us to unite around doctrines. He simply asked that we be one which means He expects us to resolve differences once we gather around Him, not around doctrines or traditions. Many years ago, I learnt from school of ministry that doctrines are absolute, experiential or interpretational. I won't delve too much into the theological intricacies of each of these segments but I must mention that absolute doctrines are what bind the church together. The absolutes are however not very many. Some examples are

- "Jesus is the Son of God and was born of the virgin Mary".
- "He was killed for the remission of our sins and through belief in His name and acceptance of His sacrificial death, we receive forgiveness of sin and total redemption".
- "He rose from the dead, ascended into heaven and is returning for those who expect Him".
- By the Holy Spirit, He dwells in every heart that has received Him.

All who wholeheartedly believe these and accept Jesus as Lord are children of God and should unite around these absolute principles. Experiential and interpretational realms are the items sparking major controversies today. Examples are
- Holy Ghost baptism evidenced through speaking in tongues
- Essentials of water baptism as being equal to salvation

- Covering of women's hair in church
- Payment of tithes
- Use of anointing oil and the list goes on.

These are not absolute terms and should be left at the level of people's convictions thus should not be subjects of division in Christ's Body. A quote from Loren Cunningham's book, *Winning God's Way* may explain this a lot more:

The Word of God in Ephesians 4 tells us we need to be diligent to preserve the unity of Spirit until someday we all attain to the unity of the faith (verses 2-13). We must agree on the basics – the divinity and Lordship of Christ, the Bible as the Word of God, the work of the cross, and other main tenets of faith. But where we disagree, we must leave it to God and keep our hearts right. Our responsibility is to do everything we can to maintain the spirit of unity – the very spirit of Jesus (John 17).

People have also tried to divide the church along political lines so that, if their denominational leader is not in agreement with another denominational leader, they loyally take sides, thus increasing the existing gaps across denominations. Paul scolded the Corinthian church for trying to segregate around apostolic workers. Some claimed allegiance to Peter, some to Paul and others to Apollos. (1 Cor 1: 10-13)

Jesus Christ is the rallying central figure in church. Any other figure that tries to play His role is a god and should be dethroned vehemently. The little gods are often times the sources of disharmony between brethren. As we have established, Christ gives us reasons to unite, not divide.

Assuredly, I say to you, whatever you bind on earth will be bound in heaven, and whatever you loose on earth will be loosed in heaven.
Matthew 18:18

One great benefit of unity is the guarantee of answer to prayers. Note here that the unity is important to enable the church collectively know the mind of God, for it is only then we can pray His will to be done. Matt 18:18 is not an open cheque to agree on just anything. Far from it! We must unite to agree with heaven's decrees, declare them as God's representatives on earth and then watch His mighty demonstration of power here on earth. Any agreement that is superficial and not in accordance with what heaven purposed will tally with what men did at the tower of Babel in rebellion against God. (Gen 11:1-9)

> *If we can bury hatchets of division and competition, we shall be positioned for greater exploits than has ever been achieved in the history of the church.*

NON-DENOMINATIONAL ARMY

As we already established in this chapter, the church Christ died for is not compartmentalised into boxes called denominations. Far from it! Denominations are man-made inventions in human efforts to institutionalise church. But today we draw thick lines of division around denominations as if God is interested in denominations. I have belonged to a denomination in which members never stopped talking about the covenant God established with the founder and by extension, the entire denomination. No doubt God established that covenant with the man, but it doesn't supersede the covenant God has with His church as a whole. God is far more interested in the health of His Body than the progress of a denomination!

In his book, *Church Shift*, Sunday Adelaja discussed the issue of denomination in an interesting manner:

Too many Christians and Christian leaders spend their energy, creativity, and precious time promoting churches instead of the kingdom. They work for the success of their church, or perhaps for a group of churches in their city, or they work for their ministry or denomination. They believe that by building churches and ministries they are building the kingdom.

I urge every reader of this book to adopt a 'One Church' mentality from now. Never think "us" and "them" in the context of church. Instead, understand that what delights the Lord Jesus is to see true believers connect with each other as siblings regardless of creed, culture, race, tongue and even doctrinal differences. The church of Christ is ONE church. Peter and Paul as Apostolic workers realised they belonged to the same church but with slightly different doctrinal inclinations. Rather than divide the church over that, they related in love and focused on the kinds of people they were called to reach – Jews and Gentiles respectively.

Let us examine another scripture:

Therefore the ungodly shall not stand in the judgment, nor sinners in the congregation of the righteous Ps 1:5

God has a congregation that is not confined within denominational walls. That needs further explanation. In the scripture above, we see that there is a congregation referred to. We are either in or out of that congregation. Membership within a denomination and active participation in religious activities do not qualify for acceptance into this congregation. Only the blood of Jesus has the potency to open the gate into the congregation, and only hands and hearts that have been washed in the blood, and remain clean, congregate with the Lord daily.

The church of the Lord has no denominational bias. This church is not just about Sunday morning meetings, and a few other meetings during the week. While these are important, there is more to Christianity. The 'congregation of the righteous' stand before God on a continuous basis. They are ever before Him in sleep and in consciousness. Have you ever wondered how God was able to reserve 7000 men in Israel as warriors of righteousness yet Elijah the mighty prophet had no inkling of it? These 7000 formed His 'righteous congregation' in their generation. Most of them wouldn't have known themselves yet the Lord kept them as His holy people in different parts of Israel. This is what He is doing in our days. There are many Christians who have not bowed to idols nor kissed them, and the Lord has His mark on them. What God has is a network of believers across the length and breadth of the earth. He doesn't have denominations. Instead, He has one church which cuts across our many denominations. That network is the 'congregation of the righteous'. That is the true church of the Lord. They express His attributes in their daily interactions with the surrounding world yet remain pure. They infiltrate their world without getting stained. That is the church Jesus died for.

I dare say that the church does not thrive on denominational rules or constitutions. She exists legitimately through the sustenance of God's Spirit and commensurate flow of His Life. The only acceptable constitution is God's Word. So church is not permitted to exclude anyone from her circle simply on the basis of non-adherence to denominational guidelines. The main problem with denominations is that they thrive on division. If as a church, we start to look across denominational walls by de-emphasising our differences, an unprecedented revival will overtake this age. If we can bury hatchets of division and competition, we shall be positioned for greater exploits than has ever been achieved in the history of the church. The driver is unity!

SIMPLICITY

Another hallmark of the church of Christ is simplicity which the Master Himself portrayed in His manner of birth, way of life, speech and general conduct. He gave birth to a simple yet extraordinary church. What an interesting paradox! How can a people so powerful and influential in spiritual realms appear so simple on the earth? Why would Jesus, Lord of the Universe make Himself of no reputation and be subject to such unimaginable humiliation by His own creation. The secret was revealed in the first two verses of Hebrews chapter 12. The key phrase is "for the joy that was set before Him".

Jesus operated in simplicity because there was reward for enduring hardship. The reward which Paul also described as a "far exceeding eternal weight of glory" outweighs the sacrifice attached to living simple lives. In the present world, it is difficult to live simply. The temptations true Christians have today are often not outright sins of immorality, lies, theft etc. Our real challenge today is the difficulty of staying simple and avoiding the ferocious traps of worldliness. In the world, every one scrambles to out-do the other and since Christians live in a real world, we are often caught in the same trap of vanity. Christians want to own better mansions than their peers. They want to drive better cars and send their children to better schools. They want to be seen as the best in the eyes of the world. Although such desires in some occasions can be induced by legitimate needs, they challenge the Lord's requirement for us to live simple unassuming lives. Let me state this clearly. The Lord desires quality lives for us but quality can come with simplicity too. Problems begin to surface when we compare our individual performances with our peers. At that stage, simplicity and moderation are often thrown out of the window. As I explained in chapter 2, Paul's subjection of his body was to address legitimate yet non-critical needs. I pray we receive grace to walk in simplicity. Sometimes we may even appear unnoticed by the world yet

> *Divine results that mesmerize the complex systems of the world are delivered through channels of simplicity.*

be seen as making impact in God's sight. May church no longer be defined by the size of our buildings and the number of cars our leaders have, or even their fame. May church not be defined by the traffic chaos and discomfort we cause our neighbours when we hold conferences and other large meetings. Instead, may we be known by the unusual power we exhibit and the simplicity accompanying the delivery of such power.

The story of David and Goliath teaches us an important lesson on simplicity. *Then he took his staff in his hand; and he chose for himself five smooth stones from the brook, and put them in a shepherd's bag, in a pouch which he had, and his sling was in his hand. And he drew near to the Philistine.* 1 Sam 17:40

In this interesting story, Goliath represents the enemy of our souls – the devil. Goliath as we see in preceding verses was decked in extremely sophisticated gadgets, representing the complexities of the world. So large was his shield that it had to be carried by an armour bearer. Similarly, our world thrives on complex technologies and processes even though those elements in themselves do not have the potency to solve all problems. Technology is good but it doesn't win the battle of the mind and does not necessarily bring peace to the soul. As David approached Goliath for his derby in battles for territories, King Saul tried to arm him with worldly military gadgets which David politely turned down. Now here is the key. David simply picked five smooth stones from the brook. How on earth could five stones match the complexity of the military might Goliath and team presented? God was teaching a lesson: His Kingdom operates through simplicity that has

God's breath. As well as deliverance comes through such measure of simplicity.

Church should function in the simple way God designed her to function. Anything short of that is an aberration of the ultimate plan of God for His church. All of the complex titles, edifices, complex organisational structures, "Sunday morning dress codes" and rigid "order of services" are products of man's intelligent inventions and oftentimes have nothing to do with God. As we see in the story of David and Goliath, simplicity gets the job done neatly. Divine results that mesmerize the complex systems of the world are delivered through channels of simplicity. No wonder Paul told the Corinthian church that God chose the weak things to confound the mighty. Also, He chose the foolish things of the world to confound the supposedly wise ones (1 Cor 1:27). Simplicity is the rule of the game!

INTEGRITY

The bride of the Lord Jesus constitutes of a holy people. Just like every other attribute mentioned so far in this chapter, this is non-negotiable and as the writer of Hebrew recorded, it is a condition to see God on judgement day (Heb 12:14). There is an interesting element of holiness. Only a tiny bit of its manifestation is seen. We can safely assume an 80/20 rule on this topic; 80% of holiness is hidden in the heart and 20% is

> *The beautiful bride of Jesus is made of people that have integrity.*

the outward action seen by men. Let us examine some scriptures to support this rule.

Who may ascend into the hill of the Lord? Or who may stand in His holy place? He who has <u>clean hands and a pure heart</u>, who has not lifted up his soul to an idol, nor sworn deceitfully.
Ps 24:3-4

God (by inspiring David) set two important conditions here. One is hidden and one can be seen. One, only Him can measure its quality (a pure heart). The other, men can join in assessing (clean hands). This is both interesting and instructive. It is for this reason Paul admonished the church in Corinth to provide things honest in the sight of God and man (2 Cor 8: 21)

In the 80/20 principle, the weighting is skewed towards the heart because of a statement Jesus made:

A good man out of the good treasure of his heart brings forth good things, and an evil man out of the evil treasure brings forth evil things. Matthew 12:35

Jesus taught here that the heart was the main issue. Once the heart can be put right, the hands will be clean too. Any attempt to clean the hands and leave the heart untouched will end in futility. This is why David said God desires truth in the inward part, and in the hidden part He shall make us know wisdom (Ps 51:6). The heart is the root of the matter, friends. The church Jesus died for have their individual hearts circumcised and their consciences purged of evil through the shedding of blood. Therefore, sin is no more the protocol of such hearts. Instead, the light of God shines in their hearts, brighter and brighter until the day of perfection.

The beautiful bride of Jesus is made of people that have integrity. I must balance this by saying the journey of faith is progressive. That means our level of integrity will keep improving as we walk with the Lord. We don't get everything right in one day but we must wax stronger daily. In other words, I must be a better Christian this year than I was last year. We must continue to move closer and closer to the Lord. As our walk with the Lord deepens, seemingly little things that didn't matter at the point of salvation become critical. We begin to pay attention to minute details of life, ensuring that we please the Lord in all areas of life. The continuous adjustment is normal for a spiritual life that is truly alive in the Lord.

PROPHETIC EDGE

The church is an embodiment of prophecy fulfilled. However, it does not end there. The church still has a huge chunk of prophecy that will be fulfilled in the future – this age and beyond. That then leads us to an important conclusion – the bride of Jesus is utterly prophetic in nature. Every true child of God has a prophetic dimension to life and must function on earth through spiritual life. This needs further clarification. I am not insinuating that all Christians must function with prophetic gifts or in the office of prophets. Instead, my submission is that every Christian must tap into divine insights God provides and live life strictly by divine order. Let us examine this prophecy about Jesus revealed by Prophet Isaiah and draw its parallel to all New Testament believers

The Spirit of the Lord shall rest upon Him, the Spirit of wisdom and understanding, the Spirit of counsel and might, the Spirit of knowledge and of the fear of the Lord. His delight is in the fear of the Lord, and He shall not judge by the sight of His eyes, nor decide by the hearing of His ears.

Isaiah 11: 2-3 This was in reference to Jesus but also applies to all believers who seek to walk in His footsteps. For a fruitful exciting spiritual journey with the Lord, natural senses must be de-emphasised. In their place, the senses of the spirit must be exercised in order to access the mind of God, discern the seasons and reign in power. The attributes of the Holy Spirit mentioned in this prophecy are phenomenal! Wisdom and Understanding; Counsel and Might; Knowledge and Fear of the Lord! Every believer walking around with these attributes will always dazzle the world. The church of Jesus Christ is full of brothers and sisters who understand their prophetic edge over the world and are harnessing the counsel of the Holy Spirit. Though they live simple lives, they are power-bearing vessels through whom God rules on earth. They are delivery channels of divine power and stewards of God's manifold grace. The prophetic dimension separates the church from the world. It is little wonder then, that Moses asked for God's presence over Israel as a distinguishing factor (Exodus 33:15-16). In the 21st century church, every believer must walk, talk and live by divine guidance because the church as a whole is organically prophetic!

> *The prophetic dimension separates the church from the world.*

PURPOSE-DRIVEN

Purpose is part of the nucleus of Jesus' church. Just like marriage between a man and a wife has purpose, Jesus is marrying the church to bring her into purpose. When God delivered Israel out of Egypt, it was to give them the opportunity to serve Him. This is the reason He was often angry at the Nation when they walked out of that purpose. Rick Warren is an authority on the subject of "purpose", so let's read what he wrote about this in his book, *The Purpose Driven Church*:

Nothing precedes purpose. The starting point for every church should be the question, "why do we exist?" until you know what your church exists for, you have no foundation, no motivation, and no direction for ministry. If you are helping a new church get started, your first task is to define your purpose......
Successful ministry is "building the church on the purposes of God in the power of the Holy Spirit and expecting the results from God.

The church of Jesus Christ is on a mission that has been defined by a purpose created in God before the foundation of the earth. We are not in church for mere fun or just to pass time. We are here for serious business; PURPOSE! And the force of purpose is propelling us towards destiny.

Together, let us examine a portion of scripture:

The trees once went forth to anoint a king over them. And they said to the olive tree, reign over us! But the olive tree said to them, should I cease giving my oil, with which they honour God and men, and go to sway over tree?

Then the trees said to the fig tree, you come and reign over us! But the fig tree said to them, should I cease my sweetness and my good fruit, and go to sway over trees?

Then the trees said to the vine, you come and reign over us! But the vine said to them, should I cease my new wine, which cheers both God and men, and go to sway over trees?

Then all the trees said to the bramble, you come and reign over us! And the bramble said to the trees, if in truth you anoint me as king over you, then come and take shelter in my shade; but if not, let fire come out of the bramble and devour the cedars of Lebanon!
Judges 9:8-15

This passage is a discourse on purpose. The trees were looking for a king and carried out their search in a very interesting manner. Let us review key elements of this search:

1. The trees began their search for a king by approaching the resourceful trees among them. The first three trees approached had something worthwhile to offer their fellow trees. They can safely be regarded as successful trees. Their lives were measured by the results they had produced over time hence their peers judged them to be of royal capability. That is instructive. The world is watching the church and as it was in the days of Daniel, they are looking out for sons of God that will dictate the pace in various spheres of life. Fruit-bearing Christians are the ones Paul wrote about in Romans 8. These are the people that will set creation free from bondage into the glorious liberty of God's children.

2. One other key feature of the three trees is that they knew their God-given purpose and were secure therein. That is extremely crucial. Their statements were noble, for example "*should I cease giving oil and sway over trees?*" Political office and its associated glamour didn't appeal to these trees. Instead, they chose to live in divine order by fulfilling purpose. The olive, fig and vine trees were not power hungry and didn't seek fame because they realised that relevance and effectiveness are both locked in purpose. This is the same with the bride of Jesus. The church is full of people who are not busy seeking relevance outside purpose. It is made up of saints who are daily discovering their potentials and releasing the sweetness God deposited in them. This makes a major difference between the church and the world. Purpose defines the lifestyles of believers and frames the choices we make as individuals.

3. We shouldn't close this brief analysis without discussing the attitude of the tree that had no real value to offer. The bramble tree does not bear fruit. The trees approached it as a last resort but because it lacked true relevance, it felt important and uttered arrogant speech against Lebanon's cedar. This reflects the attitude of people that have not found their purpose in

> *Through the church, God expresses His love and deep affection for mankind*

life. They are arrogant at any taste of power. They are often the loudest even though they have no solution to offer their immediate environment. Anyone that practices the "bramble" way of life is not a representative of God's Kingdom. As we have already established in this chapter, His kingdom functions effectively through simplicity.

THE VISIBLE INVISIBILITY

For since the creation of the world his invisible attributes are clearly seen, being understood by the things that are made, even His eternal power and Godhead, so that they are without excuse.
Romans 1:20

As we have mentioned already, the church of the Lord expresses Him on the earth. They have the rare privilege of accessing His mind and revealing it on the earth. Paul describes it as God's *invisible attribute being clearly seen*. What an irony! If I am to paraphrase that statement, it would be "*The attributes of the invisible God are clearly seen.....*" This is what only the church can accomplish. We are God's hands, voice, feet etc here on earth. Through the church, God expresses His love and deep affection for mankind. He also expresses his holiness, wrath, forgiveness and other attributes that make Him God. No wonder then, that Paul said **God makes manifest the savour of His knowledge through us in everyplace** (2 Cor 2:14). The collective church is God's expressive vessel on the earth.

In that scripture (Rom 1:20), we see that there is a compelling reason God does this – so that His power remains undeniable. The world will have no excuse when they stand before God on judgement day because the church was visibly present and the world saw her light. The world can see the attributes of God through the church because those attributes are understood by God's creation – firstly in human beings but even beyond, into plants and animals. The eternal power and Godhead is however expressed most prominently through His church, that the world may have no excuse. Friends, the church of Jesus in an undeniable force dominating the earth today and even though she walks in simplicity, her presence cannot be ignored. Jesus' beautiful bride is that manifestation of His glory and visible presence on the earth. By divine design, the church is salt of the earth and therefore cannot lose relevance on earth.

> *Prayers of faith revolve around God, not our needs.*

PRAYER

The importance of prayer for the church cannot be over-emphasised. It is pivotal in establishing God's reign on the earth. And that is why Jesus taught His disciples to pray that God's will be done on earth as it is already done in heaven. Let's examine Watchman Nee's exposition of the Lord's prayer from his book, *God's Eternal Plan*:

The Bible shows us what prayer is. First, God has a need; He has a purpose. Second, He puts this purpose within man through the Holy

Spirit so that man feels this need as well. Third, man responds by uttering this purpose back to God through prayer. Fourth, God does His work and accomplishes this purpose. That is the meaning of prayer.

The Lord's Prayer as a sample of prayer shows something important – it is largely God-centred with little emphasis on needs. That speaks volumes. God does not expect us to fill our prayers with long lists of requests. Prayers of faith revolve around God, not our needs. The church spends more time kissing the Lord and appreciating Him. Prayer starts with intense worship and ends with the same. Prayer time is the time to extol God's lofty virtues, not a time to scream out marching instructions on what we want done in our lives. The church of the Lord Jesus understands this, and worships Him instantaneously at any given opportunity.

CHRIST-CENTRED MEETINGS

The beautiful bride of the Lord Jesus gathers to Him when they meet. Jesus through His Holy Spirit presides over their meetings and He expresses His mind through such meetings. I once read a heart-warming testimony of how a brother got saved at one of such believers' meetings. This man came in unsaved but as the meeting progressed, everyone present shared testimonies of how they had seen the Lord throughout that week. As they spoke, the brother cried out in desperation that he too wanted to know this Jesus. Such is the power of Christ-centred meetings. God's Life readily flows and evangelism is effortless.

Friends, as I wrap up this chapter, I share an article I recently wrote for a Christian magazine in Ireland:

Tribute to a special people

The 21st Century is experiencing an unusual phenomenon. A unique breed of people is gradually beginning to take this dispensation by storm. While the world looks on, an unstoppable force is gathering momentum. As time rolls away, a people of unusual strength, honour and dignity continue to mature in the background, waiting for the appointed time of full-blown manifestation. That time has come.

Here are some key features that indicate the remarkable difference this special people connote:

• They are people of unusual courage. People that are fearless right in the face of adversity. Seemingly daunting tasks present them with the opportunity to excel. They scale heights that intimidate kings. They occupy territories that the mighty avoid. Princes and nobles yearn endlessly in vain to decipher their wisdom and strength. What a special people!

• The people I refer to are deeply in love with themselves. This is uncommon because their love is real and selfless. This love transcends emotions, feelings and is unrestricted by culture, creed or race. They speak up for one another, defending each other. Their unwritten code of operation is "one for all, all for one", with the cord binding them outweighing natural family ties. What a special people!

• Their confidence stuns the world, especially when they declare that there is hope for a better life after this feeble world fades away. These people breathe, dream, talk and live hope. They are hope personified yet the world can't understand them. What a special people!

• In days of lack or abundance, joy and peace remain their hallmark. With heads always raised up high, they celebrate at ease. Success for them is not measured in material acquisitions but in the contribution they make to mankind. Greatness for them is defined in the highest level of service. They don't compare and contrast material possessions. Instead their good works reflect their true riches. What a special people!

• These people do things right. They are ever uncompromising in their stand for what is true and pure even when an expensive price tag is attached. Theirs is a journey of being true to inherent conscience, and utmost integrity is their watchword. What a special people!

• And one more characteristic of this important species; they have an invisible King. He rules them as one people. His will is their command and they are willing to surrender to a King they cannot see or touch. They love Him passionately even though they only sense Him deep within their hearts. And more interesting, He plans to marry them at a date set in future. To the world, this is insanity. To my peculiar people, it is faith. What a special people!

As the finish line rapidly draws close, one reality becomes increasingly clear - the best is yet to come. Having gone through thick and thin together, they prepare to finally meet their King in the most glamorous way of all time. A date is set in divinity for this glorious event.

Ladies and gentlemen, this discourse is to honour a people that I love simply because the Master has loved them eternally. The church of the Living God is marching on! What a special people!

By Muyiwa Oguntoyinbo, originally written for Splendour Magazine – Spring 2010 edition

Chapter 6

To whom shall we go?

But Simon Peter answered Him "Lord, to whom shall we go? You have the words of eternal life. Also we have come to believe and know that You are the Christ, the Son of the living God. John 6: 68-69

This is the concluding chapter of this book. You may have read this book wondering the next step to take especially if you have been convicted about certain aspects of the book. Let me state clearly that all I discuss in this chapter are recommendations from a brother. Ultimately, you need God's Spirit to lead you in His planned course for your life. Only God has the blueprint.

Let us examine Peter's address to Jesus in the passage above. This was spoken at a time disciples were taking a walk from Jesus. These men and women could no longer handle the strangeness of this Man's message. They seemed to prefer the religious comfort zone of the Pharisees rather than launch into the depth of liberty the Messiah came to offer. Since Jesus is not motivated by crowd, their departure didn't intimidate Him. Instead, His immediate reaction was to check if the twelve core disciples would also depart. This led to Peter's timely response, a reflection of unflinching allegiance.

There are a few things to note about Peter's expression:

1. All believers that come to the Lord must have only one option – Jesus, and no back-up! Marriage vows adopted by the church are probably the best illustration of the level of our commitment to the Lord. We are married to Jesus and Him alone!
2. Eternal life is the key element missing in the world. With that life comes peace, joy and other wonderful attributes.
3. Jesus' role as Christ and son of the living God positions Him as the only One qualified to release this life to as many as believe in Him.

Having established these therefore, let us truly come to Jesus and abandon our lives in His hands. Enough of church tradition and outward displays of religion! Let us truly come to the Lord Jesus, the giver of life and embrace the eternal life that He freely supplies. It is time to say "no" to church politics, "no" to vain religion and "no" to all non-kingdom **practices**. May we receive grace to truly embrace the Lord Jesus, the only One to whom we may go.

If you are deeply involved in traditional church practice and this book strikes a chord in your spirit, please pray and ask the Lord for direction on the next step to take. I do not recommend that you immediately leave your church because this may not be God's plan for you. Instead, arm yourself with the truth of God's word and as Peter, the Apostle admonished, be ready to give a reason for the hope that is in you.

Here is another important recommendation. If the Lord will have you remain in your present church, do not sit passively anymore. Cry out against Life-draining traditions you observe. Be prepared to be disliked or even hated but speak up as God's representative always and be an emblem of sincere love. This is not to encourage controversies. I agree with a pastor who recently said that a critical spirit is sign of a false ministry. Do not set out to merely criticise. Pray for your church leaders but when they err, be vocal in correcting them lovingly. As it was said of Jesus, let the zeal of the Lord's house consume you. Be an icon of truth because the One you represent is Truth, and He lives in you!

I expect this book has caused some explosions in your mind. You most certainly have issues you agree or disagree with.
As I mentioned in the introduction, I am subject to my brethren. Please raise your thoughts to me on **muyiwa@muyiwaoguntoyinbo.com** or join my blog on **www.muyiwaoguntoyinbo.com/tbbBlog** and let's rub minds together. May we receive His truth gracefully as He continues to unveil His eternal plan for His Beautiful Bride.